Second Workshop on Economics and Natural Language Processing (ECONLP 2019)

Hong Kong, China
4 November 2019

ISBN: 978-1-7138-0080-4

EMNLP-IJCNLP 2019

ECONLP — Economics and Natural Language Processing

Proceedings of the Second Workshop on Economics and Natural Language Processing (ECONLP 2019)

November 4, 2019
Hong Kong, China

Introduction

Welcome to ECONLP 2019! After launching the first Workshop on Economics and Natural Language Processing (ECONLP) at ACL 2018 in Melbourne, Australia, the second ECONLP workshop is held at EMNLP-IJCNLP 2019 in Hong Kong, China, on November 4, 2019.

This workshop reflects the increasing relevance of natural language processing (NLP) for regional, national and international economy, both in terms of already operational language technology products and systems, as well as newly emerging methodologies and techniques as a response to new requirements at the disciplinary intersection of economics and NLP. The focus of the workshop will be on the many ways how NLP influences business relations and procedures, economic transactions, and the roles of human and computational actors involved in commercial activities using natural language as primary communication mode.

The main topics ECONLP addresses include (definitely not excluding other areas of relevance for the broad workshop theme)

- NLP-based (stock) *market analytics*, e.g., prediction of economic performance indicators (trend prediction, performance forecasting, etc.), by analyzing verbal statements of enterprises, businesses, companies, and associated legal or administrative actors

- NLP-based *product analytics*, e.g., based on social and mass media monitoring, summarizing reviews, classifying and mining complaint messages and other (non)verbal types of customer reactions to products or services

- NLP-based *customer analytics*, e.g., client profiling, tracking product/company preferences, screening customer reviews or complaints, identifying high-influentials in economy-related communication networks

- NLP-based *organization/enterprise analytics* (e.g., tracing and altering social images of organizational actors, risk prediction, fraud analysis, predictive analysis of annual business, sustainability and auditing reports)

- Analysis of *market sentiments and emotions* as evident from consumers' and enterprises' verbal behavior and their communication strategies about products, services or market performance

- *Competitive intelligence* services based on NLP tooling

- Relationships and interactions between *quantitative (structured) economic data* (e.g., contained sales databases and associated time series data) and *qualitative (unstructured verbal) economic data* (press releases, newswire streams, social media contents, etc.)

- *Organizational information management* based on the content-based assembling, packaging and archiving of verbal communication streams in organizations/enterprises (emails, meeting minutes, business letters, internal reporting, etc.)

- *Credibility and trust models* for business agents involved in the economic process (e.g., as traders, sellers, advertisers) extracted from text/opinion mining their current communication as well as legacy data

- *Deceptive or fake information* recognition related to economic objects (such as products, advertisements, etc.) or economic actors (such as industries, companies, etc.), including opinion spam targeting or emanating from economic actors and processes

- Verbally fluent *software agents* (chat bots for counseling, sales and marketing) as reliable actors in economic processes serving business interests, e.g., embodying models of persuasion, information biases, fair trading

- *Enterprise search engines* (e-commerce, e-marketing) involving NLP analytics

- *Consumer search engines*, market monitors, product/service recommender systems involving NLP analytics

- *Client-supplier interaction platforms* (e.g., portals, helps desks, newsgroups) and transaction support systems based on written or spoken natural language communication

- *Multi-media and multi-modality interaction platforms*, including written/spoken language channels, triggering or supporting economic processes

- Specialized modes of *information extraction and text mining* in economic domains, e.g., temporal event or transaction mining

- *Information aggregation* from economy-related discourse, from and across single sources (e.g., review summaries, automatic threading)

- *Text generation* in economic domains, e.g., review generation, complaint response generation

- *Ontologies for economics*, lexicons for the economy domain or adaptation of general-domain lexicons for economic NLP – acquisition, maintenance or update of such terminological resources

- *Corpora and annotations policies* (guidelines, metadata schemata, etc.) for economics-related NLP

- *Economy-specific text genres* (business reports, sustainability reports, auditing documents, product reviews, economic newswire, business letters, law documents, etc.) and their usage for NLP

- Dedicated *software resources* for economic NLP (e.g., NER taggers, sublanguage parsers, pipelines or end-to-end systems for processing economic discourse)

Two types of papers were solicited for the ECONLP 2019 workshop:

- Long papers (8+1 pages) should describe solid results with strong experimental, empirical or theoretical/formal backing,

- Short papers (4+1 pages) should describe work in progress where interesting novel, yet still preliminary results have been worked out.

We received this year 17 submissions (from which 1 was withdrawn during the review process), and based on a rigorous review process, we accepted 5 of them as long papers, 3 as short papers and rejected 8 from the remaining 16 papers. Accordingly, the acceptance and rejection rate was equally 50%. The acceptance/rejection ratio amounts to 1.0.

Compared with ECONLP 2018, the first workshop on Economics and Natural Language Processing, we received one more submission, decreased the acceptance rate from 64% to 50% (conversely, we increased the rejection rate from 36% to 50%); the acceptance/rejection ratio fell from 1.9 in 2018 to 1.0 this year. Also the proportion of long papers relative to short ones increased substantially this year, up from 2 (2018) to 5 for long papers and down from 7 (2018) to 3 for short papers in 2019. Cautiously, one might interpret this change as an indication that work in this field gets deeper and riper.

Overall, the theme of this workshop seems to become more and more attractive for a wide range of neighbouring scientific communities, including NeurIPS, IJCAI, KDD, and SIGIR. Without aiming for completeness, the list below enumerates some major events with a similar thematic scope in 2019:

- *Robust AI in FS 2019 — Workshop on Robust AI in Financial Services: Data, Fairness, Explainability, Trustworthiness, and Privacy @ NeurIPS 2019*, Vancouver, B.C., Canada, December 2019

- *FinNLP & FinSDB 2019 — First Workshop on Financial Technology and Natural Language Processing (FinNLP) with a Shared Task for Sentence Boundary Detection in PDF Noisy Text in the Financial Domain (FinSBD) @ IJCAI-2019*, Macao, China, August 2019

- *ADF 2019 — Second Workshop on Anomaly Detection in Finance @ KDD 2019*, Anchorage, Alaska, USA, August 2019

- *eCom 2019 — 3rd SIGIR ACM SIGIR Workshop on eCommerce @ SIGIR 2019*, Paris, France, July 2019

- *FNP 2019 — Second Financial Narrative Processing Workshop @ NoDaLiDa 2019*, Turku, Finland, September 2019

Hence, ECONLP might constitute the institutional hub for gathering the contributions of the ACL-affine NLP community dealing with a wide range of economic topics.

Last but not least, we want to thank those colleagues who submitted their work to our workshop and hope that their efforts will strengthen a process of productive and sustainable activities in this exciting interdisciplinary domain. In particular, we also want to thank our PC members whose thorough and timely reviews were the basis for properly selecting the best-quality papers presented at this workshop. Finally, we hope the attendants of the workshop will enjoy the presentations and discussions in Hong Kong.

The organizers of ECONLP 2019

Udo Hahn
Véronique Hoste
Zhu (Drew) Zhang

Organizers:

Udo Hahn	Friedrich-Schiller-Universität Jena, Germany (Chairman)
Véronique Hoste	Ghent University, Belgium
Zhu (Drew) Zhang	Iowa State University, Ames, IA, USA

Program Committee:

Sven Buechel	Friedrich-Schiller-Universität Jena, Germany
Hsin-Hsi Chen	National Taiwan University, Taipei City, Taiwan
Paulo Cortez	University of Minho, Guimarães, Portugal
Sanjiv Ranjan Das	Santa Clara University, CA, USA
Brian Davis	Maynooth University, Ireland
Flavius Frasincar	Erasmus Universiteit, Rotterdam, The Netherlands
Petr Hájek	Univerzita Pardubice, Czech Republic
Allan Hanbury	Technische Universität Wien, Austria
Qing Li	Southwestern University of Finance and Economics, Sichuan Sheng, China
Pekka Malo	Aalto University, Finland
Julian J. McAuley	University of California, San Diego, CA, USA
Viktor Pekar	Aston University, Birmingham, England, U.K.
Paul Rayson	Lancaster University, England, U.K.
Samuel Rönnqvist	University of Turku, Finland
Sameena Shah	S&P Global Ratings, New York City, NY, USA
Kiyoaki Shirai	Japan Advanced Institute of Science and Technology (JAIST), Nomi, Ishikawa, Japan
Padmini Srinivasan	University of Iowa, Iowa City, IA, USA
Amanda Stent	Bloomberg LP, New York City, NY, USA
Heiner Stuckenschmidt	Universität Mannheim, Germany
Chuan-Ju Wang	Academia Sinica, Taipei City, Taiwan
Wlodek W. Zadrozny	University of North Carolina, Charlotte, NC, USA
Ming Zhou	Microsoft Asia Research, Beijing, China

Invited Speaker:

Marco Enriquez	Division of Economic and Risk Analysis, U.S. Securities and Exchange Commission (SEC), Washington, D.C., USA

Keynote talk: NLP for Financial Regulation

Marco Enriquez

Division of Economic and Risk Analysis, U.S. Securities and Exchange Commission (SEC),
Washington, D.C., USA

Abstract[1]

Narrative disclosures have been long-standing components of regulatory requirements (e.g., the U.S. SEC's requirement for corporate issuers to file 10-Ks). As the length of these disclosures grow in size and as the number of registrants increase, however, manual review of these corpora has become impractical or infeasible. Hence, there has been increasing interest in Natural Language Processing (NLP) among financial regulators across the world. In this talk I cover use-cases of NLP to aid in regulatory workflows: from processing to risk assessment and surveillance. I also discuss main challenges that regulators have faced to systematically deploy NLP capabilities in production environments. Finally, I detail shortcomings of current NLP technologies for financial regulation, and areas for future research and improvement.

---

[1]The Securities and Exchange Commission disclaims responsibility for any private publication or statement of any SEC employee or Commissioner. This talk expresses the author's views and does not necessarily reflect those of the Commission, the Commissioners, or members of the staff.

Table of Contents

Conference Program

Monday, November 4, 2019

9:00–9:30   *Introduction to the ECONLP workshop*
Udo Hahn

9:30–10:40   SESSION 1: FINANCIAL EVENT EXTRACTION

9:30–10:00   *Extracting Complex Relations from Banking Documents*
Berke Oral, Erdem Emekligil, Seçil Arslan and Gülşen Eryiğit

10:00–10:20   *Financial Event Extraction Using Wikipedia-Based Weak Supervision*
Liat Ein-Dor, Ariel Gera, Orith Toledo-Ronen, Alon Halfon, Benjamin Sznajder, Lena Dankin, Yonatan Bilu, Yoav Katz and Noam Slonim

10:20–10:40   *A Time Series Analysis of Emotional Loading in Central Bank Statements*
Sven Buechel, Simon Junker, Thore Schlaak, Claus Michelsen and Udo Hahn

10:40–11:00   *Coffee Break 1*

11:00–12:30   SESSION 2: FINANCIAL FORECASTING AND PREDICTION

11:00–11:30   *Forecasting Firm Material Events from 8-K Reports*
Shuang (Sophie) Zhai and Zhu (Drew) Zhang

11:30–12:00   *Incorporating Fine-grained Events in Stock Movement Prediction*
Deli Chen, Yanyan Zou, Keiko Harimoto, Ruihan Bao, Xuancheng Ren and Xu Sun

12:00–12:30   *Group, Extract and Aggregate: Summarizing a Large Amount of Finance News for Forex Movement Prediction*
Deli Chen, Shuming Ma, Keiko Harimoto, Ruihan Bao, Qi Su and Xu Sun

12:30–14:00   *Lunch Break*

14:00–14:45   *Invited Talk: NLP for Financial Regulation*
Marco Enriquez (Division of Economic and Risk Analysis, U.S. Securities and Exchange Commission)

14:45–15:35   SESSION 3: MISCELLANEOUS TOPICS

14:45–15:15   *Complaint Analysis and Classification for Economic and Food Safety*
João Filgueiras, Luís Barbosa, Gil Rocha, Henrique Lopes Cardoso, Luís Paulo Reis, João Pedro Machado and Ana Maria Oliveira

15:15–15:35   *Annotation Process for the Dialog Act Classification of a Taglish E-commerce Q&A Corpus*
Jared Rivera, Jan Caleb Oliver Pensica, Jolene Valenzuela, Alfonso Secuya and Charibeth Cheng

15:35–16:00   *Coffee break 2*

16:00–16:30   Feedback round from the audience - future directions of ECONLP

16:30–18:00   POSTER PRESENTATIONS

Extracting Complex Relations from Banking Documents

Berke Oral[1,2], Erdem Emekligil[1], Seçil Arslan[1], and Gülşen Eryiğit[2]

[1]R&D and Special Projects, Yapı Kredi Technology
[2]Department of Computer Engineering, Istanbul Technical University
{*erdem.emekligil, secil.arslan*}*@ykteknoloji.com.tr*
{*oralbe, gulsen.cebiroglu*}*@itu.edu.tr*

Abstract

In order to automate banking processes (e.g. payments, money transfers, foreign trade), we need to extract banking transactions from different types of mediums such as faxes, e-mails, and scanners. Banking orders may be considered as complex documents since they contain quite complex relations compared to traditional datasets used in relation extraction research. In this paper, we present our method to extract intersentential, nested and complex relations from banking orders, and introduce a relation extraction method based on maximal clique factorization technique. We demonstrate 11% error reduction over previous methods.

1 Introduction

Despite recent efforts for digitalization in banking domain, formal letters (such as orders, petitions, demands or complaints) still remain as one of the main communication media in corporate banking. A mid-to-large scale bank receives millions of orders in a year, most of which are money transfer requests. Reading and manually processing those documents require significant amount of human labour. Moreover, since these documents require specialized knowledge to be interpreted, employment and education of trustable personnel is often difficult. This situation makes the automatization of the process crucial.

Automatic processing of banking documents is an Information Extraction (IE) task, where one seeks to extract structured information from semi-structured or unstructured texts. This is usually conducted with pipelined processes. The one used in this study depicted in Figure 1. The first step is to extract entities of interest from raw text, in our case is extracted via Optical Character Recognition (OCR) system. This can be done with Named Entity Recognition (NER) algorithms or pattern

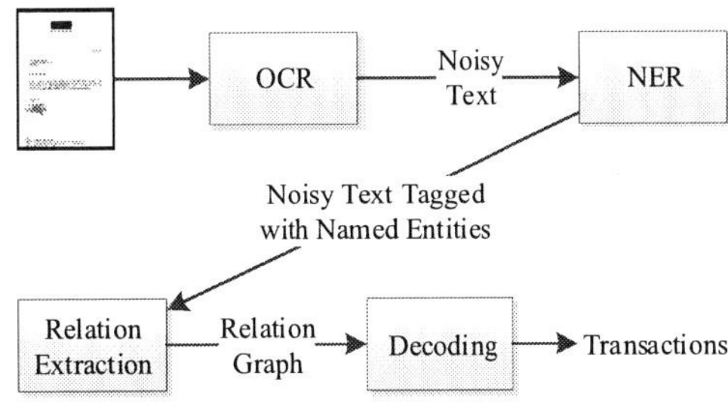

Figure 1: Information extraction pipeline.

based methods. Secondly, semantic relations between extracted entities are predicted with Relation Extraction (RE) algorithms. Finally, semantic structures are constructed on top of the relations as higher order structures such as templates or events.

NER is an important step for many Natural Language Processing (NLP) tasks. It is a widely researched area, and current state-of-the-art algorithms (Lample et al., 2016) give satisfactory results in most situations. RE is considered as a linguistically higher order task compared to NER, and proposed algorithms are often tailored to problems in hand. Majority of research in this area is focused on extracting binary relations. Although there are some research dealing with complex relations (McDonald et al., 2005; Peng et al., 2017), work on nested complex relations as in the case of banking transactions is scarce.

In this paper, we focus on money transfer requests as the major process type in banking orders. Within these documents, we seek to extract *transactions* as our structured information of interest. Each order may contain one or more transactions, which are made of sender and receiver account numbers, names, bank information as well as details of transaction process such as the transfer amount and its currency type. In order for a transaction to be valid, its sender, receiver and pro-

Proceedings of the Second Workshop on Economics and Natural Language Processing, pages 1–9
Hong Kong, November 4. ©2019 Association for Computational Linguistics

cess details should be clearly defined. Thus, in our system, we abstract these real-world entities as three main *divisions* of a transaction: sender, receiver, and process details. Each of these divisions contains required (emphasized with bold font in Figure 2) or optional *slots*. Sender and Receiver divisions must either include an Account Number or IBAN (having either one of these is enough to address the account). Process Details must contain transfer Amount and its Currency.

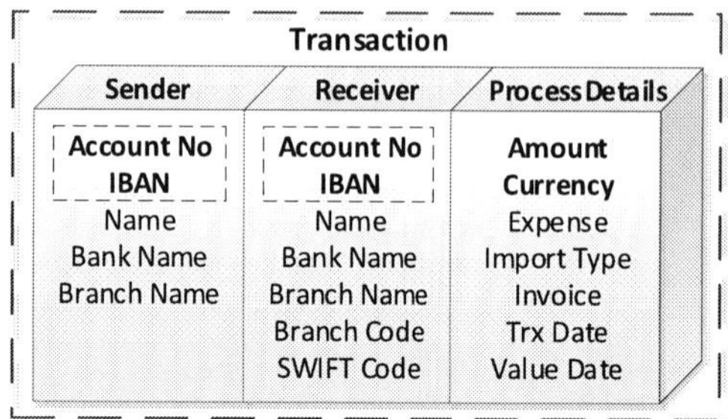

Figure 2: Divisions of a transaction and their slots.

Slots of the divisions should be filled with named entities extracted from a document. Named entities related to the same slot might have been stated multiple times by the author in different places of the document. For example, the name of the account holder may occur within both the body text and the signature part. Additionally, a single named entity may carry information for multiple slots belonging to different transactions. For example, multiple money transfer orders might have been given from a single sender account, hence an entity holding the sender IBAN should be linked to different transaction slots. Figure 3 provides such a sample document with two transactions. Private information were masked on the figure, and extracted entities were specified with colored boxes.

In this paper, we focus on the relation extraction and the decoding stages of the pipeline introduced in Figure 1.[1] We propose a method that can automatically extract transaction information from banking documents by forming nested complex relations using a relation graph. Our algorithm first predicts binary relations between entities. This forms an undirected graph, where nodes are entities, and edges are predictions. On this graph, the algorithm performs series of maximal

---

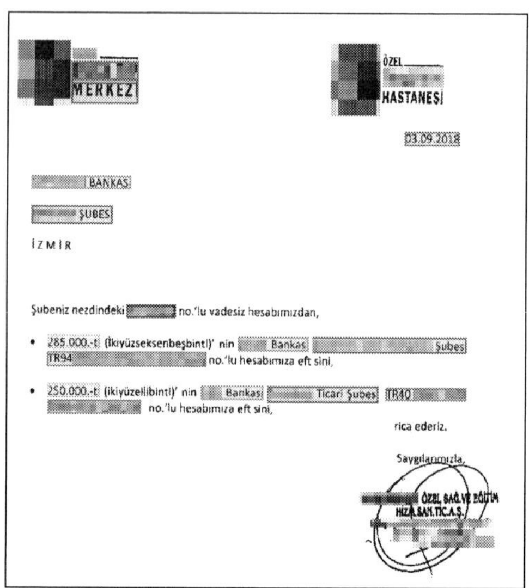

Figure 3: A sample money transfer order document with two different transactions provided in separate lines starting with bullets. Best viewed in color.

clique factorization operations to form transactions.

In Section 2, we discuss the previous work on intersentential complex relations. In Section 3, we describe a transaction extraction method that uses maximal cliques in a predicted relation graph to extract complex relations. Lastly, we discuss comparable approaches to our method in Section 4, and give our remarks in Section 5.

2 Related Work

In early IE systems (Chinchor, 1998), extracting complex relations (i.e database entries, templates) was mostly accomplished with rule based approaches. To the best of our knowledge Chieu and Ng (2002) was first to extract complex relations from binary relations using maximal clique approach. In biomedical domain, McDonald et al. (2005) extended this approach by adding predicted probabilities from a trained classifier. Using geometric mean of the relation probabilities in cliques, they selected highest scoring cliques as complex relations. Rather than using maximal cliques, Wick et al. (2006) used a clustering algorithm to construct complex relations. They trained a classifier that computes similarity score between two clusters. Starting from singletons, their clustering algorithm built relation tuples.

Event extraction also deals with complex relations. In this task, algorithms often detect a trigger

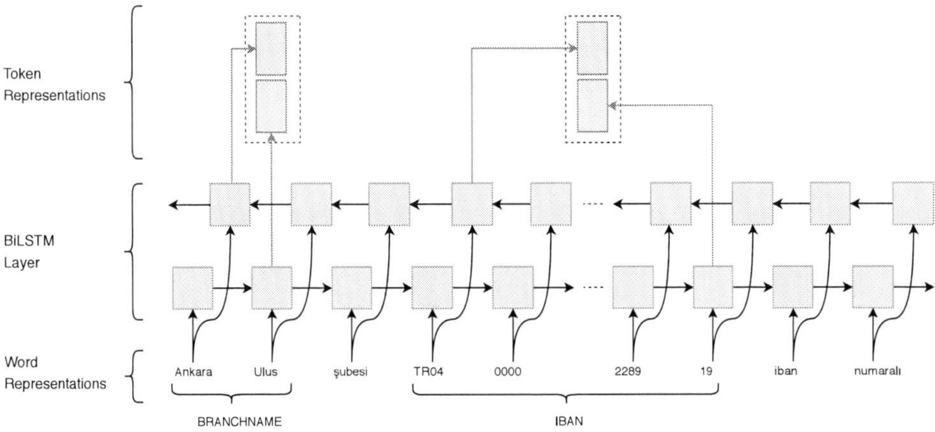

Figure 4: Entity representations

word for an event, then using the trigger word and its relations, arguments of an event are filled. Our approach to transaction extraction is analogous to event extraction. In our case, the trigger is a group of amount entities. An interesting approach in this area is the use of dependency parsing algorithms as means of complex relation extraction (McClosky et al., 2011; Sprugnoli and Tonelli, 2017; Wang et al., 2018). In literature, closest work to ours is by Şahin et al. (2018), which uses a non-projective transition based parser to extract transactions from banking documents.

Although most of the research in relation extraction literature focused on binary relations from single sentences, n-ary and document level relation extraction has become increasingly popular in recent years. Notably, Peng et al. (2017) proposes a graph LSTM architecture, which runs on two directed acyclic graphs constructed from syntactic dependency trees of sentences. In these graphs, syntactic roots of consequent sentences are linked together. This allows the algorithm to capture syntactic features between entities in proximate sentences. Later, their model predicts n-ary relations among fixed number of entities. Jia et al. (2019) create entity representations from different discourse sizes (document, paragraph, sentence) and predicts relations for each entity tuple in a document. In this approach, as the number of entities in document increases, possible n-ary relations will explode (2^n), which makes this approach for n-ary relation extraction computationally not feasible. However, they merge multiple mentions of a same entity (e.g same gene mentioned in different paragraphs or sentences) into

one representation, which reduces the number of entities in the relation extraction step. They argue that this step makes n-ary relation extraction computationally affordable. In our case, the number of required slots, the complexity of relation types, and the existence of multiple mentions referring to the same transaction slots (occurring under very distinct surface forms also due to OCR errors) make the task even more challenging.

3 Method

We propose a method to extract transactions from banking documents, given a sequence of words and their named entity types.[2] It first creates a representation for each entity within the text, then predicts an undirected relation for each entity pair. This creates a fully-connected graph that our decoding algorithm uses to construct transactions.

3.1 Relation Extraction

In this section, we describe the architecture and the training details of our relation extraction model. Each banking document is provided as a single sequence to our model, which predicts a relation type for each entity pair. We use a BiLSTM to create contextual representations for our entities and two entity representations are concatenated then fed into a multilayer perceptron (MLP) with three hidden layers to predict relations. This creates an undirected graph which is represented by matrix $R^{N \times N}$ where N is the number of entities in a graph. We calculate the cross entropy loss for

---

[2]Our named entity types are named as the same with slot names shown in Figure 2.

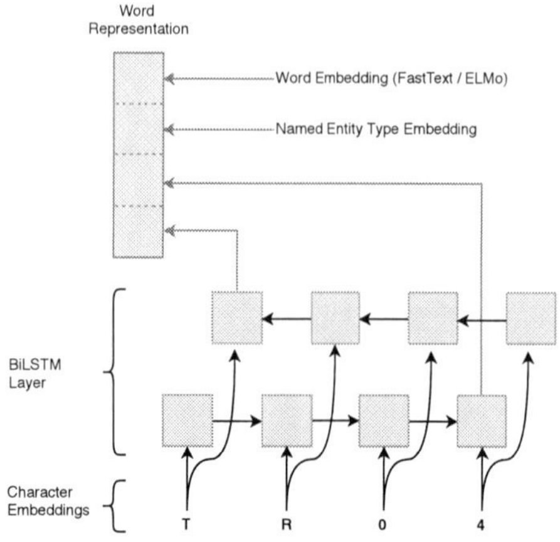

Figure 5: Word representations

each element of the matrix and take their sum as document loss.

In banking documents, entities are often formed of multiple words (e.g., branch name, IBAN entities in Figure 4). Therefore, we need to derive the entity representations from multiple word representations. As the overall entity representations, we use the concatenation of forward and backward LSTM outputs at the entity boundaries (right boundary token for the forward pass and left boundary token for the backward pass). Figure 4 visualizes our entity representation. Two dotted rectangles on the top represent the embeddings for the two entities branch name and IBAN composed of 2 and more than 4 tokens respectively. The arrows coming to the dotted rectangles depict the representations extracted from the entity boundaries.

Each word in our model is reprensented as the concatenation of three vectors: pretrained word embeddings, character level word representations, and named entity type embeddings (Figure 5). We pre-trained our word-embeddings via both Fast-Text (Bojanowski et al., 2016) and ELMo (Peters et al., 2018) by using a corpus of 626M words collected from banking domain. Using the standard parameters, both models were trained for 10 epochs. FastText embeddings were loaded into a lookup table. To represent out of vocabulary (OOV) words in FastText embeddings we used zero vector with same of the embedding dimension. Our documents contain plenty of numerical values crucial for our task such as account numbers, amounts, dates etc. Those appear diverse surface forms, yielding to rare occurrence counts.

We used a word transformation algorithm in order to represent them with FastText. The algorithm is used if the number of letters in a word is less than or equal to the half of the word length. It replaces the word with a token specifying the count of letters (L), digits (D) and punctuation characters (O) it contains (see Table 1 for examples). Because ELMo creates word embeddings from characters, we did not need to apply this transformation for ELMo representations. Character level representation of words are also created again by a BiLSTM layer similar to Lample et al. (2016). Both character embeddings and named entity type embeddings are initialized randomly and learned during training.

Word	Token
22/05/2019	<L0D8O2>
TR04	<L2D2O0>
10,000	<L0D5O1>

Table 1: Examples of word transformation algorithm

We implemented our models using Tensorflow framework. Number of words in documents and number of characters in words vary for each instance. We used mini-batching during training. Each word and character padded to longest element in the mini-batch with padding tokens so that each instance has the same sized vector. Similarly, since the number of entities in the documents also varies, we padded the relation matrices in the mini-batches with padding entities and NONE relations. During training, we did not use the padded cells in loss calculation. For optimization we used Adam (Kingma and Ba, 2015) algorithm with learnin rate of 1e-3. We used annealing of 0.9 after every epoch. For regularization, we used dropout (0.5) at the BiLSTM inputs and before each hidden layer in MLP.

3.2 Relation Structure

In order to correctly extract the transactions within a money transfer order document, one needs to correctly determine the transaction count and fill their slots (Figure 2). This kind of complex structures may be formulated as binary relations (McDonald et al., 2005). We defined an undirected relation structure unique to solve money transfer orders where multiple transactions may occur within a single document and some entity types (e.g., name, bankname) are shared between sender and receiver divisions of a transaction. We defined 5

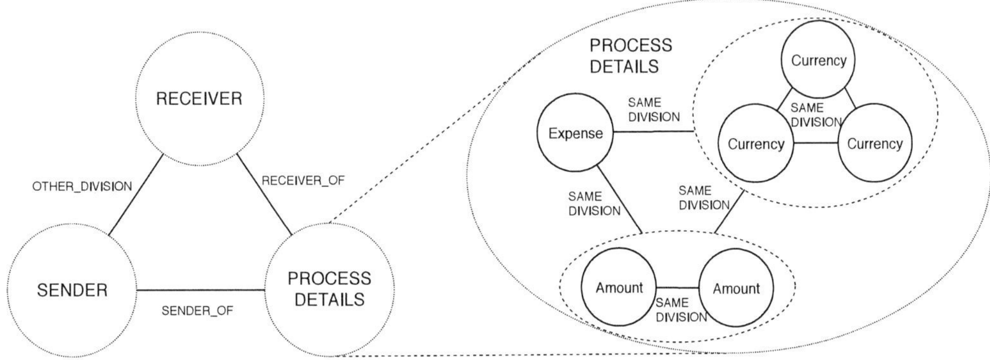

Figure 6: An example relational graph containing a transaction.

different relation labels (detailed in Table 2) in order to distinguish the divisions to which the entities belong within a transaction. For instance, entities that are connected with RECEIVER_OF relation are either in receiver or process details divisions. Since possible entity types that reside in sender and process details divisions do not intersect (Figure 2), we can distinguish entities of these two divisions although the relations are undirected. Below, we describe our algorithm to decode multiple transactions within an order. In Figure 6, we provide a visualization for the relations within a single transaction. For simplicity, we provide only the abstract divisions on the left side of the figure and the relations between them meaning that entities belonging to these divisions will be related to the entities of the other division with the mentioned relation types. On the right side of the figure, we zoom into one of the divisions (process details) where entities belonging to a same division are connected to each other with SAME_DIVISION relation type. As explained in the previous sections, named entities occurring within the docu-

ments might have been stated multiple times by the author in different places of the document. The figure depicts (with dashed ellipses) a scenario where the same currency is repeated (maybe with slight surface form differences) 3 times within the order and the amount is repeated 2 times. One should keep in mind that this is just a visualization and we actually keep this fully-connected undirected graph as a binary relation matrix $R^{N \times N}$.

3.3 Extracting Transactions

The first step of our decoding algorithm is to determine the number of possible transactions. In order to achieve this, the decoding algorithm creates a sub-graph from amount entities. Since the entities of different transactions are expected to be connected with NONE relation type, each maximal clique of this sub-graph can be said to belong to different transactions.[3] However mistakes in relation extraction process complicate this. Missing or extra edges between nodes (i.e., entities in our case) can result in extra cliques, where many of their nodes are shared. Algorithm uses cardinality of maximal cliques to discard possibly wrong ones. It compares cliques to each other and eliminates the smaller clique if it has a node that intersects with larger clique. If two cliques has same the cardinality while sharing a node, it randomly eliminates one of the cliques. The result of this process is an unconnected set of cliques which are treated as the roots of separate transactions.

Once the transaction root nodes are discovered, i.e the amount slots (the process details division) for each transactions are determined, it becomes

Relation Type	Description
NONE	Entities are not in the same transaction
SAME_DIVISION	Entities are in the same division
OTHER_DIVISION	One entity is in Sender while other is in the Receiver division
RECEIVER_OF	One entity is in Receiver while other is in the Process Details division
SENDER_OF	One entity is in Sender while other is in the Process Details division

Table 2: Possible relation types and their description

---

[3] Although some slots may be shared between transactions, it is a convention that amounts are specified explicitly for each transaction. In fact, in our data there exist no amount entities that are shared between transactions.

possible to fill the other slots by using the relation graph. In a perfect world, where all relations are extracted correctly, this slot filling is very trivial: each entity value will be written to a slot regarding to the relation type of that entity to the root node. Due to the errors propagating from the relation extraction stage, we need a decoding algorithm to fill out the missing parts of the transactions. To fill each slot, our algorithm first looks up all the entities that has matching named entity types and creates a sub-graph from these if they are connected to the amount. For example, if we aim to fill the sender division's bank name slot for a transaction, we will extract all bank name entities connected with SENDER_OF relation to the amount entities of that transaction. This time, we select a maximum clique of the entities connected with a SAME_DIVISION relation and fill the slots with their values.

Only transactions that contains required slots (sender and receiver division's account number or IBAN slots, process details division's amount, and currency slots) are considered as valid transactions. In the last step of our decoding algorithm, we pruned the outputs transactions that is not containing those required slots.

With the above decoding algorithm, it is possible that re-occuring entities (with exact or different surface forms) are assigned to a single slot. One may use a post-processing stage to select the best entity value for a slot.[4]

4 Experimental Results

4.1 Dataset

Our dataset contains 3500 Turkish banking documents with a total of 4102 transactions. In order to represent different types of layouts, the dataset is collected such that each document is from a different customer.[5] The dataset contains 51,396 entities and 1.17 transactions per document, 6.7% percent of them contains multiple transactions. On average, there are between 1.18 to 2.23 entities per slot depending on the slot type.

The documents are in image format since they are received via fax, scanner or email channels. They contain misrecognized characters, extra or missing characters or spaces, incorrect token sequences and so on due to noisy images and OCR errors. In our experiments, we randomly selected 600 of these documents (containing 730 transactions in total) as our test set and 400 of them as the validation set.

4.2 Experiments and Discussions

Our algorithm predicts a relation type for each entity pair in a document. This creates a relation graph which is represented as an $N \times N$ matrix where N is the number of entities. To evaluate relation extraction performance, we used F1 measure. Since the relations are undirected, we used only the upper triangles of relation matrices in our evaluations. Since the cells on the diagonal line of the relation matrix are always expected to contain SAME_DIVISION relations, they are excluded from the evaluations. Table 3 gives relation extraction scores of our model both with FastText and ELMo embeddings. The dataset contains many rarely occurring words due to noisy OCR outputs, especially in numerical tokens and proper nouns. We observe that such rare words are handled better by ELMo.

Relation Label	Count	Model w/ FastText	Model w/ ELMo
NONE	16786	74.18	84.97
SAME_DIVISION	17948	88.56	93.10
OTHER_DIVISION	13000	97.08	95.95
RECEIVER_OF	13333	90.26	92.43
SENDER_OF	15156	97.27	96.49
Macro Avg		89.47	92.59
Micro Avg		88.88	92.35

Table 3: F1 scores of binary relation extraction step

In order to measure the performance of our transaction extraction stage, we used a slot level entity matching evaluation. Entities occurring in both predicted and gold slots were counted as true positives, the remaining entities within a predicted slot were counted as false positives, and the missed entities of a gold slot were counted as false negatives. Since each page may contain multiple transactions, while evaluating the predicted transactions, we first needed to match them with gold ones. We computed a similarity score for each predicted-gold transaction pair in a document and selected highest scoring pairs. The similar-

---

[4]The post-processing is crucial for our task since the input source of our data is OCR and the data is noisy. For example, we use an IBAN validator at this stage.

[5]Customers would usually prefer to use their own document layout (templates) for their consecutive transaction orders yielding documents with similar layouts.

		Rule Based	Trans. Based	Model w/ FastText	Model w/ ELMo
Sender	P	80.32	87.21	94.61	**96.05**
	R	60.19	72.42	81.13	**82.65**
	F1	68.60	79.10	87.34	**88.79**
Receiver	P	78.49	87.07	91.99	**92.45**
	R	56.33	69.00	81.74	**83.39**
	F1	65.29	76.91	86.47	**87.58**
Details	P	87.56	91.39	94.63	**95.33**
	R	56.14	69.21	85.35	**87.25**
	F1	68.00	78.56	89.70	**91.04**
Overall	P	82.86	89.21	93.86	**94.59**
	R	57.32	70.18	83.35	**85.10**
	F1	67.35	78.41	88.22	**89.50**

Table 4: Slot level entity matching macro average scores grouped by divisions.

ity score was geometric mean of entity matching scores (F1) between required slots (sender's and receiver's account numbers and IBAN, amount, and currency of transaction). We set a rule where predicted transactions could not match with gold transactions if the similarity score was 0, or they were already matched with other predicted transactions. Unmatched predicted transactions were counted as *wrong*, and all of their entities were counted as false positives during slot level evaluation. Similarly unmatched gold transactions were counted as *missed*, and their entities were counted as false negatives. Table 4 provides slot level entity matching scores grouped by divisions and as overall.

We compare our method with two models: the rule based and the dependency based approaches from Şahin et al. (2018). The rule based method is derived from banking conventions and some basic patterns. It chooses the first seen account entity as sender and remaining ones as receiver. Other entities are set using a similar logic that also considers their proximity to divisions. For instance, it can select the closest currency entity to the amount as its currency.

We also adapted Şahin et al. (2018)'s dependency parsing method to our data, which resulted in increased number of entity and relation types. Since, our dataset contains more entity types (14 vs 7 in Şahin et al. (2018)), during the adaptation, we needed to add more relation types to the ones in the original study. This approach uses a transition based non-projective dependency parsing model (Nivre et al., 2009) to attach account numbers to

the root of a dependency tree as Sender/Receiver, and related entities (name, bank name, etc.) to Sender/Receiver account numbers. Amounts are attached to receivers while currency and other process details are attached to amounts. This approach makes an assumption that each document can only have one sender. Since, each receiver carries all the unique entities of a transaction, multiple transactions can easily be constructed.

Rule-based method cannot relate more than one entity with a slot. As a result, it performs marginally worse in recall. To correctly fill a slot, it is enough to find one true entity in the document. However, since we are working on a text coming from an OCR system, entities are often misspelled. Having more than one entity in a slot is advantageous for post-processing steps.

Our model clearly outperforms both the rule-based and the dependency parsing methods. The use of ELMo embeddings gives consistent improvements in both precision and recall. Although the dependency parsing model achieves satisfactory results in precision, its performance in recall is poor. We argue that this is due to the way the dependency trees are constructed in Şahin et al. (2018). Each dependent may be attached to one head, therefore in slots that have multiple true entities (e.g in cases where sender's name stated multiple times), entities are expected to be attached to each other with a directed dependency relation (called "*SAME*") according to their occurrence order. Then, the first entity within this order is expected to be attached to its true head. According to our view, this is kind of a unnecessarily strict grammar for the semantic problem in hand. In our investigations over the predicted outputs, we see that the transition based parser struggle to detect correct order for *SAME* relations, thus degrading its parsing accuracy.

Figure 7 shows the average slot level score difference between our model (FastText) and transition-based dependency parsing model. In slots where there are multiple entities, the difference in recall is consistently higher than the cases where we have one entity for a slot. It is also interesting that precision scores of the two methods are very similar. However, in empty slots, dependency parsing model has much higher number of false positives: 702 in the dependency parsing model vs. 304 in the FastText and 192 in the ELMo models. We interpret this as LSTMs better ability to

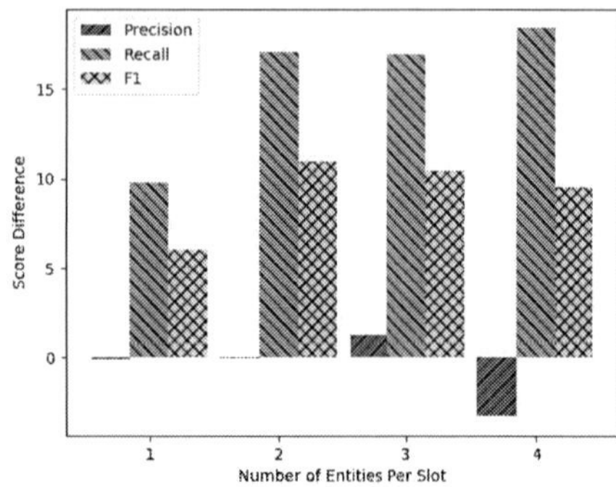

Figure 7: Score difference between our model (w/ Fast-Text embeddings) and transition based parser model. Horizontal axis shows number of possible entities for a slot.

# Errors	Rule Based	Trans. Based	Model w/ Fasttext	Model w/ ELMo
0	74	372	454	490
1	52	43	47	40
2	81	70	52	39
3	62	17	21	13
4	80	4	11	7
5	63	5	9	4
6+	91	12	4	13
# Matched	503	539	601	606
# Missed	227	191	129	124
# Wrong	67	64	27	13

Table 5: Number of entity matching errors in predicted&matched transactions. Number of *matched*, *missed*, and *wrong* transactions are also given in bottom rows.

learn semantics of pages.

We also counted the number of entity matching errors in order to evaluate the quality of predicted and matched transactions. Table 5 provides these statistics (in the upper block) as well as the numbers of missed and wrong transactions of each model (in the lower block). Unlike in the slot level evaluation, performance of the rule based model is not dramatically worse than the other methods based on the matched transaction counts, but the predicted transactions have lower quality. Rule based model could predict only 14.7% of the transactions with no error in any of their slots, while this ratio is much higher in other models. Similarly to our slot level evaluations, our models give better performance than the other two methods, while the use of ELMo embeddings provides consistent improvements.

5 Conclusion

In this paper, we introduced a method to extract transactions from banking documents. The method uses BiLSTM based deep neural network to predict relations between each entity pairs, and creates a relation graph. From this graph, our decoding algorithm constructs a series of sub-graphs and applies maximal clique factorization to determine number of transactions and fill their slots. We demonstrated that our method is more accurate at predicting transactions and their slots than previously proposed methods. Moreover, It has a higher recall rate on slots with multiple entity candidates. This allows the use of excess entities in post-processing steps, which can mitigate the mistakes of OCR system.

Acknowledgments

This work is supported by The Scientific and Technological Research Council of Turkey with the project no TEYDEB 3180571. We would like to thank our colleagues Mehmet Yasin Akpınar, Cemil Cengiz, Deniz Engin, and Tuğba Pamay for their valuable discussions and support.

References

Piotr Bojanowski, Edouard Grave, Armand Joulin, and Tomas Mikolov. 2016. Enriching word vectors with subword information. *CoRR*, abs/1607.04606.

Hai Leong Chieu and Hwee Tou Ng. 2002. A maximum entropy approach to information extraction from semi-structured and free text. In *Eighteenth National Conference on Artificial Intelligence*, pages 786–791, Menlo Park, CA, USA. American Association for Artificial Intelligence.

Nancy A. Chinchor. 1998. Overview of MUC-7. In *Seventh Message Understanding Conference (MUC-7): Proceedings of a Conference Held in Fairfax, Virginia, April 29 - May 1, 1998*.

Robin Jia, Cliff Wong, and Hoifung Poon. 2019. Document-level n-ary relation extraction with multiscale representation learning. *CoRR*, abs/1904.02347.

Diederik P. Kingma and Jimmy Ba. 2015. Adam: A method for stochastic optimization. In *3rd International Conference on Learning Representations, ICLR 2015, San Diego, CA, USA, May 7-9, 2015, Conference Track Proceedings*.

Guillaume Lample, Miguel Ballesteros, Sandeep Subramanian, Kazuya Kawakami, and Chris Dyer. 2016. Neural architectures for named entity recognition. In *Proceedings of the 2016 Conference of the North American Chapter of the Association for Computational Linguistics: Human Language Technologies*, pages 260–270, San Diego, California. Association for Computational Linguistics.

David McClosky, Mihai Surdeanu, and Christopher D. Manning. 2011. Event extraction as dependency parsing. In *Proceedings of the 49th Annual Meeting of the Association for Computational Linguistics: Human Language Technologies - Volume 1*, HLT '11, pages 1626–1635, Stroudsburg, PA, USA. Association for Computational Linguistics.

Ryan McDonald, Fernando Pereira, Seth Kulick, Scott Winters, Yang Jin, and Pete White. 2005. Simple algorithms for complex relation extraction with applications to biomedical IE. In *Proceedings of the 43rd Annual Meeting of the Association for Computational Linguistics (ACL'05)*, pages 491–498, Ann Arbor, Michigan. Association for Computational Linguistics.

Joakim Nivre, Marco Kuhlmann, and Johan Hall. 2009. An improved oracle for dependency parsing with online reordering. In *Proceedings of the 11th International Conference on Parsing Technologies (IWPT'09)*, pages 73–76, Paris, France. Association for Computational Linguistics.

Nanyun Peng, Hoifung Poon, Chris Quirk, Kristina Toutanova, and Wen-tau Yih. 2017. Cross-sentence n-ary relation extraction with graph lstms. *Transactions of the Association for Computational Linguistics*, 5:101–115.

Matthew E. Peters, Mark Neumann, Mohit Iyyer, Matt Gardner, Christopher Clark, Kenton Lee, and Luke Zettlemoyer. 2018. Deep contextualized word representations. *CoRR*, abs/1802.05365.

R. Sprugnoli and S. Tonelli. 2017. One, no one and one hundred thousand events: Defining and processing events in an inter-disciplinary perspective. *Natural Language Engineering*, 23(4):485–506.

Shaolei Wang, Yue Zhang, Wanxiang Che, and Ting Liu. 2018. Joint extraction of entities and relations based on a novel graph scheme. In *Proceedings of the 27th International Joint Conference on Artificial Intelligence*, IJCAI'18, pages 4461–4467. AAAI Press.

Michael Wick, Aron Culotta, and Andrew McCallum. 2006. Learning field compatibilities to extract database records from unstructured text. In *Proceedings of the 2006 Conference on Empirical Methods in Natural Language Processing*, pages 603–611, Sydney, Australia. Association for Computational Linguistics.

Gözde Gül Şahin, Erdem Emekligil, Secil Arslan, Onur Ağın, and Gülşen Eryiğit. 2018. Relation extraction via one-shot dependency parsing on intersentential, higher-order, and nested relations. *Turkish Journal of Electrical Engineering & Computer Sciences*, 26(2):830–843.

Financial Event Extraction Using Wikipedia-Based Weak Supervision

**Liat Ein-Dor, Ariel Gera, Orith Toledo-Ronen, Alon Halfon, Benjamin Sznajder,
Lena Dankin, Yonatan Bilu, Yoav Katz and Noam Slonim**
IBM Research, Haifa, Israel

Abstract

Extraction of financial and economic events
from text has previously been done mostly
using rule-based methods, with more recent works employing machine learning techniques. This work is in line with this latter approach, leveraging relevant Wikipedia sections
to extract weak labels for sentences describing
economic events. Whereas previous weakly
supervised approaches required a knowledge-
base of such events, or corresponding financial figures, our approach requires no such additional data, and can be employed to extract
economic events related to companies which
are not even mentioned in the training data.

1 Introduction

Event Extraction from text (Hogenboom et al.,
2011; Ritter et al., 2012; Hogenboom et al., 2016)
has been the subject of active research for over two
decades (Allan et al., 2003). Detection and extraction of finance-related events have mostly focused
on events described in news articles, which are
likely to impact stock prices. In particular, previous work has sought to extract descriptions of
events pertaining to a specific company, and analyzed how such events correlate with measures of
that company's stock (price, volatility etc.). While
much of the literature has focused on the prediction of stock prices (e.g., Ding et al., 2015; Xie
et al., 2013), it is recognized that predicting future
stock movements is a formidable challenge (see
e.g. Merello et al., 2018); still, there are use-cases
that might benefit from business-related event extraction from news.

One promising direction is enhancing the
finance-related research performed by finance analysts. Such research typically requires reviewing
a large body of news data under severe time con-
straints. We propose an automatic system for high-
lighting meaningful company-related news events
that are likely to deserve the analyst's attention.

Work on economic event extraction often defines an ad-hoc taxonomy of events, and what con-
stitutes an 'important event' for one might not
be considered as such for another. For instance,
the CoProE event ontology (Kakkonen and Mufti,
2011) includes events such as patent issuance and
delayed filing of company reports, which are not
considered by Du et al. (2016); similarly, while
CoProE consider earnings estimates by analysts as
events, Jacobs et al. (2018) examine instead analyst buy ratings and recommendations.

Outlining a comprehensive list of event types
seems futile. For example, if a company's
databases are hacked, this is certainly an influential event; but compiling an explicit and exhaustive
event taxonomy that is sufficiently fine-grained to
include all events such as this one is doomed to
fail. At the same time, a formal event hierarchy is
not necessarily required from an analyst's perspective. The strength of an automated system comes
from the ability to process a large volume of news
data and detect events of interest; automatically
classifying these events into types is probably of
secondary importance to an expert in the field.

Thus, our focus here is on a binary classification
problem that is not type-based. This presents an
interesting challenge, since the aim is not capturing the characteristics of predefined event types,
but rather capturing general properties of relevant
events.

The common NLP approach for economic event
extraction has mostly made use of hand-crafted
rules and patterns (Feldman et al., 2011; Arendarenko and Kakkonen, 2012; Xie et al., 2013;
Hogenboom et al., 2013; Ding et al., 2014, 2015;
Du et al., 2016). However, creating and maintaining such rules is time consuming, and further
seems less suitable for our scenario, where no set

Proceedings of the Second Workshop on Economics and Natural Language Processing, pages 10–15
Hong Kong, November 4. ©2019 Association for Computational Linguistics

of underlying event types (which give rise to such rules) is assumed. Hence, here we follow a different, more flexible approach, that relies on a robust statistical learning framework for identifying relevant events. In particular, we adopt a supervised learning approach for identifying events related to a given company, and suggest to train a sentence-level classifier for this purpose. Given sentences from news articles discussing the company, the classifier aims to identify sentences containing events that would be of interest to the analyst. Since the sentences come from articles discussing the company, our main focus is on determining whether a sentence conveys an event worth considering, and not on ascertaining that it is related to the company.

Learning a supervised model requires annotated data. The standard approach for obtaining annotated data involves human annotation, which requires a substantial effort and limits the size of the data, which in turn may hinder the results. One way to overcome this problem is using weak supervision (Zhou, 2017), where labelled data is generated automatically using heuristics rather than manual annotation. Although such data may be noisier and less precise compared to standard labelled data, it enables to create much larger amounts of data at a significantly lower cost. Here we rely on content from Wikipedia to automatically generate a weakly-labelled sentence dataset for company events. We report experimental results that demonstrate the potential merit of our approach.

2   Related Work

Arendarenko and Kakkonen (2012) relied on a collection of hand-crafted detection rules in order to recognize 41 distinct company-related event types, and Du et al. (2016) used about 600 distinct patterns to cover 15 business event types.

More recently, machine-learning techniques were considered for this task. Jacobs et al. (2018) frame the problem as a multi-class classification task. They define a taxonomy of 10 event types, in addition to a "no-event" class, and 7 companies of interest, and rely on manual annotation to train a sentence-level multi-class classifier. Testing several classifiers, they show that a linear SVM classifier attains the best results for most event types. While the current paper also adopts a supervised learning sentence-level approach, here the data is constructed based on weak labels, and the task is framed as a type-independent binary classification problem.

Rönnqvist and Sarlin (2017) used weak supervision in the context of financial events, focusing on bank distress events. They consider 101 banks for which 243 such events, and their date, are known. They then extract 386K sentences referring to these banks, and consider a sentence as describing a distress event if there is a matching event in the knowledge base mentioning the same bank and occurring near the publication date of the article from which the sentence was extracted. This approach requires a large knowledge-base of specific events, which is not readily available when moving from a confined event type (i.e. bank distress) to a diverse space of events. In this work we suggest a weak-label approach that aims to encompass a variety of relevant entities, event types and event occurrences.

3   Data

We used two types of datasets, one which is created automatically based on weak labels, and another which is based on manual annotation.

3.1   Weakly labelled datasets - Wikipedia

We leverage the content of Wikipedia articles describing companies as a source of influential events in the company's chronology.

In order to automatically identify 'positive' sentences which likely describe noteworthy events, we rely on two observations: 1. Such events tend to appear within specific Wikipedia sections. 2. Sentences beginning with a date, specifically the *date-pattern* $['On/In/By/As\,of' + month + year]$, often describe an event. Thus, we manually created a lexicon of words which tend to appear in the titles of event-prone sections. A section whose title contains one of the following words is defined as an *event-section*: history, creation, leadership, corporate, acquisitions, growth, finance, financial, lawsuits, litigation, legal.

Given a company C, we select from its Wikipedia article all sentences appearing in an *event-section* and starting with a *date-pattern*. We remove the opening date and mark the sentences as positive examples with respect to C. All sentences which do not start with a *date-pattern* and are not in an *event-section* are considered as negative. To balance the dataset, we enforce an equal number of positive and negative examples by discarding sentences from the larger set. In addition, since many positive examples begin with either the company's name or the words "the company", we aim to balance the two classes in terms of sentences containing these patterns. The rest of the negative examples are chosen at random.

The procedure described above was used to create two datasets. The first, $S\&P\text{-}wiki$, is generated from Wikipedia articles of the companies on the S&P-500 index. A larger dataset, $Extended\text{-}wiki$, was later generated from Wikipedia articles of companies traded in one of five major stock exchanges[1], yielding 3.8K companies in total.

Each dataset was split into train and test sets based on dates - all positive examples up to 2018 are in the training set, and all those from 2019 are in the test set. Negative examples, which have no date attached, were split at random between the two sets, keeping the number of negative and positive examples equal within each set. Table 1 indicates the statistics of the resulting datasets, which will be released as part of this work.

3.2 Manually labelled dataset - SentiFM

To the best of our knowledge, the only manually annotated dataset for event detection in news articles is SentiFM (Jacobs et al., 2018). This dataset contains manual annotations of sentences into 10 predefined financial event types. However, this dataset is designed to solve a slightly different problem from the one explored in this paper. SentiFM was constructed in the context of a multiclass classification problem, whereas here we deal with a binary problem. Namely, we are not interested in event types, and do not assume there is a closed set of underlying types describing the events of interest. Indeed, it is possible that an event of interest might not be included in the SentiFM taxonomy, and hence a corresponding sentence would be labeled as negative. Despite these differences, we sought to examine how a classifier trained on the SentiFM data would perform on our task. To this end, we created a *binary* version of SentiFM, by considering all 'no-event' sentences as negative examples, and all event types as positives. We kept the original train/test split (see Table 1) and denote this data set as $SentiFM\text{-}binary$.

Model	Train	Test
$SentiFM\text{-}binary$	8943 (0.2)	443 (0.2)
$S\&P\text{-}wiki$	6130 (0.5)	272 (0.5)
$Extended\text{-}wiki$	20074 (0.5)	908 (0.5)

Table 1: Data size (number of sentences) for the three models. The numbers in parenthesis indicate the percentage of positive samples.

Company	Articles	Sentences
Apple Inc.	438	10627
Facebook	302	6827
Qualcomm	120	3332
FedEx	67	1808
Anadarko Petroleum	91	1478
Xilinx	53	569
MGM Resorts International	32	463
Accenture	24	442
Allergan	35	421
Campbell Soup Company	27	307

Table 2: Number of articles and sentences in the $News\text{-}2019$ evaluation data.

3.3 2019 News Sentences - $News\text{-}2019$

In order to evaluate methods for detecting company-related events within news data, we compile a set of sentences from news articles. Specifically, we selected the 10 S&P companies with the largest number of events from 2019 mentioned in their Wikipedia page (see Table 2). For each company, we retrieved all articles from 2019 on Seeking Alpha[2] that contained the company name in their title. We assume that this set of articles provides a good coverage of the company's events of interest during 2019. We applied sentence-splitting[3] on the retrieved articles, keeping only sentences 10-50 tokens long.

4 Experiments

The datasets described in Section 3 were used to train three event detection models. All classification models are based on BERT (Devlin et al., 2018), which has shown state-of-the-art results in many NLP tasks. We use a single-sentence input, and fine-tune the classifier with the $SentiFM\text{-}binary$, $S\&P\text{-}wiki$ and $Extended\text{-}wiki$ data sets. Henceforth, we will use these

---

[1] Hong Kong, London, NASDAQ, NYSE and Tokyo; Extracted via Wikipedia categories of these exchanges.

[2] seekingalpha.com; Transcriptions of company earning calls were filtered out due to their unique nature.

[3] using the NLTK library

names to refer to their corresponding BERT models. We use the BERT$_{\text{BASE}}$ model configuration, with maximum sequence length of 256, batch size of 16, dropout rate of 0.1 and learning rate of 5e-5. Each model was fine-tuned over 3 epochs, using a cross-entropy loss function.

4.1 Initial model evaluation

We first evaluate the performance of the three models on their corresponding test sets. As shown in Table 3, all models reach high performance when tested on the same type of data used in training. Next, we evaluate these models on the $Extended\text{-}wiki$ test set (see Table 3). Notably, although less than 15% of the companies in $Extended\text{-}wiki$ are in $S\&P\text{-}wiki$, the latter model exceeds 90% precision and recall over the $Extended\text{-}wiki$ test data. This suggests that the model is also able to detect events for companies that were not seen in training.

4.2 Identifying Wikipedia events in the news

Ultimately we are interested in the ability to detect events in the target domain of *news articles*. To validate performance over this domain, we used sentences from $News$-2019 and cross-referenced them with company events from Wikipedia. Specifically, we manually extracted events from 2019 from the Wikipedia pages of the companies in Table 2. For each event, we asked 3 annotators to mark all sentences from $News$-2019 which mention this event. In total, 26 of the Wikipedia events were mentioned in at least one sentence.

We then applied each of the three models to all the news sentences, and kept only the sentences that were classified as positive by the model. For each model, we measure the event recall rate as the fraction of Wikipedia events which are mentioned in at least one positively-classified sentence.

As expected, the recall rates of the Wikipedia-based models over the news data (Table 4) are lower than those achieved over Wikipedia data. This may be due to the difference in writing style between the two sources. Notably, even though $SentiFM\text{-}binary$ was trained on news data, its recall is the lowest among the three models. This may be attributed to the mismatch between the event types in $SentiFM$ and those in Wikipedia.

Sorting the positively-classified sentences by their model score, we also measure the average rank of the highest-scored mention of each

Model	Precision	Recall	F1
$SentiFM\text{-}binary$	0.97	0.96	0.96
$S\&P\text{-}wiki$	0.97	0.92	0.94
$Extended\text{-}wiki$	0.93	0.95	0.94
$SentiFM\text{-}binary$	0.80	0.30	0.44
$S\&P\text{-}wiki$	0.92	0.93	0.93
$Extended\text{-}wiki$	0.93	0.95	0.94

Table 3: Model performance on its test set (upper) and on the $Extended\text{-}wiki$ test set (lower)

Model	Recall	Avg. Rank
$SentiFM\text{-}binary$	0.38	153
$S\&P\text{-}wiki$	0.73	21
$Extended\text{-}wiki$	0.77	19

Table 4: Model performance for identifying 26 Wikipedia events in the news data.

event (Table 4). Clearly, the Wikipedia reference events do not fully cover all company-related events that occurred over this time period. Still, since we presume events mentioned in Wikipedia are relatively significant, we expect a good event-detection model to rank them among its top predictions.

4.3 Identifying general events in the news

So far our experiments considered only Wikipedia events. However, there are likely numerous company-related news events that are not necessarily mentioned in the company's Wikipedia page. Thus, the question remains whether the Wikipedia-based models are able to detect such events as well. To this end, the top 20 model predictions of $SentiFM\text{-}binary$ and $Extended\text{-}wiki$ for the companies in Table 2 were annotated by three co-authors of this work. The guidelines were to determine whether a given sentence contains information which may have influence on the companys stock price, as such events presumably deserve the attention of a finance analyst. The annotation process was composed of two stages. First, each sentence was annotated by two labelers. Then, the sentences on which there was disagreement between the labelers (21% of the sentences) were annotated by a third annotator. Average agreement between the initial two annotators was 0.45 (Cohen's Kappa).

Table 5 shows the precision of the two models, compared to a baseline of randomly-selected sen-

Model	Precision
Random sentences	0.28
SentiFM-binary	0.70
Extended-wiki	0.74

Table 5: Average precision over the top-20 predicted events in the news evaluation data.

tences. The *Extended-wiki* model outperforms *SentiFM-binary*.

Finally, we wanted to analyze the diversity of events captured by the two models. For this purpose, we looked at the distribution of unique tokens in the top 200 predictions of each model, after filtering out stop words and the companies appearing in the list of Table 2. We sorted the remaining tokens by their frequency from highest to lowest, and computed the cumulative frequency as a function of the number of unique tokens. Figure 1 indicates that the top candidates of *Extended-wiki* capture a richer vocabulary than *SentiFM-binary*, which is dominated by a smaller group of tokens. For example, 20% of the tokens are covered by the 36 and 19 most frequent tokens in *Extended-wiki* and *SentiFM-binary*, respectively. Moreover, despite their similar precision values, the population of events captured by the two models is quite different - the overlap between their top candidates is less than 10% (18 out of 200 examples). This observation suggests that the models are complementary, and that there is potential benefit to combining them.

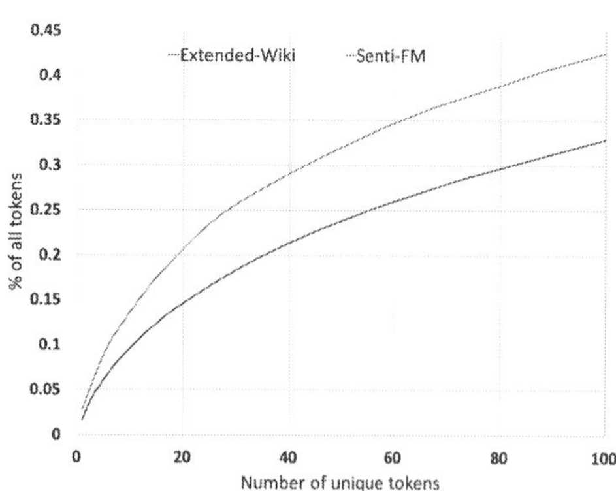

Figure 1: Cumulative token frequency over top model predictions.

5 Discussion

This paper focused on detecting 'important' events in news articles, related to a specific company. We suggested to leverage information contained in Wikipedia to create weakly-labelled data, and proved the usefulness of the resultant classifier for the desired task. We believe that the results can be further improved by finding additional sources for weak-labels, e.g. by exploiting information from relevant knowledge bases.

The potential coverage of relevant events can be increased by retrieving articles which do not necessarily include the name of the considered company in their title. Extending our framework to pinpoint noteworthy events for a particular company, mentioned in articles that are not focused on that company, is a natural direction for future research. Such an extension will require adapting the weak labelled data and the corresponding classifiers to cope with an environment in which sentences are not necessarily relevant to the company.

References

James Allan, Jaime G Carbonell, George Doddington, Jonathan Yamron, and Yiming Yang. 2003. Topic detection and tracking pilot study final report.

Ernest Arendarenko and Tuomo Kakkonen. 2012. Ontology-based information and event extraction for business intelligence. In *Proceedings of the 15th International Conference on Artificial Intelligence: Methodology, Systems, Applications*.

Jacob Devlin, Ming-Wei Chang, Kenton Lee, and Kristina Toutanova. 2018. Bert: Pre-training of deep bidirectional transformers for language understanding. *arXiv preprint arXiv:1810.04805*.

Xiao Ding, Yue Zhang, Ting Liu, and Junwen Duan. 2014. Using structured events to predict stock price movement: An empirical investigation. In *Proceedings of the 2014 Conference on Empirical Methods in Natural Language Processing (EMNLP)*, pages 1415–1425, Doha, Qatar. Association for Computational Linguistics.

Xiao Ding, Yue Zhang, Ting Liu, and Junwen Duan. 2015. Deep learning for event-driven stock prediction. In *Proceedings of the 24th International Conference on Artificial Intelligence*, IJCAI'15, pages 2327–2333. AAAI Press.

Mian Du, Lidia Pivovarova, and Roman Yangarber. 2016. Puls: natural language processing for business intelligence. In *Proceedings of the 2016 Workshop on Human Language Technology*, pages 1–8. Go to Print Publisher.

Ronen Feldman, Benjamin Rosenfeld, Roy Bar-Haim, and Moshe Fresko. 2011. The stock sonarsentiment analysis of stocks based on a hybrid approach. In *Twenty-Third IAAI Conference*.

Alexander Hogenboom, Frederik Hogenboom, Flavius Frasincar, Kim Schouten, and Otto Van Der Meer. 2013. Semantics-based information extraction for detecting economic events. *Multimedia Tools and Applications*, 64(1):27–52.

Frederik Hogenboom, Flavius Frasincar, Uzay Kaymak, and Franciska De Jong. 2011. An overview of event extraction from text. In *DeRiVE@ ISWC*, pages 48–57. Citeseer.

Frederik Hogenboom, Flavius Frasincar, Uzay Kaymak, Franciska De Jong, and Emiel Caron. 2016. A survey of event extraction methods from text for decision support systems. *Decision Support Systems*, 85:12–22.

Gilles Jacobs, Els Lefever, and Véronique Hoste. 2018. Economic event detection in company-specific news text. In *EcoNLP workshop at the 56th Annual Meeting of the Association for Computational Linguistics*, pages 1–10. Association for Computational Linguistics.

Tuomo Kakkonen and Tabish Mufti. 2011. Developing and applying a company, product and business event ontology for text mining. In *Proceedings of the 11th International Conference on Knowledge Management and Knowledge Technologies*.

Simone Merello, Andrea Picasso Ratto, Yukun Ma, Luca Oneto, and Erik Cambria. 2018. Investigating timing and impact of news on the stock market. In *2018 IEEE International Conference on Data Mining Workshops*.

Alan Ritter, Oren Etzioni, Sam Clark, et al. 2012. Open domain event extraction from twitter. In *Proceedings of the 18th ACM SIGKDD international conference on Knowledge discovery and data mining*, pages 1104–1112. ACM.

Samuel Rönnqvist and Peter Sarlin. 2017. Bank distress in the news: Describing events through deep learning. *Neurocomputing*, 264:57–70.

Boyi Xie, Rebecca Passonneau, Leon Wu, and Germán G Creamer. 2013. Semantic frames to predict stock price movement. In *Proceedings of the 51st annual meeting of the association for computational linguistics*, pages 873–883.

Zhi-Hua Zhou. 2017. A brief introduction to weakly supervised learning. *National Science Review*, 5(1):44–53.

A Time Series Analysis of Emotional Loading in Central Bank Statements

Sven Buechel♣ Simon Junker◇ Thore Schlaak◇ Claus Michelsen◇ Udo Hahn♣

♣ Jena University Language & Information Engineering (JULIE) Lab
Friedrich-Schiller-Universität Jena
Fürstengraben 27, D-07743 Jena, Germany
`https://julielab.de/`

◇ German Institute for Economic Research (DIW)
Mohrenstraße 58, D-10117 Berlin, Germany
`https://www.diw.de`

Abstract

We examine the affective content of central bank press statements using emotion analysis. Our focus is on two major international players, the European Central Bank (ECB) and the US Federal Reserve Bank (Fed), covering a time span from 1998 through 2019. We reveal characteristic patterns in the emotional dimensions of valence, arousal, and dominance and find—despite the commonly established attitude that emotional wording in central bank communication should be avoided—a correlation between the state of the economy and particularly the dominance dimension in the press releases under scrutiny and, overall, an impact of the president in office.

1 Introduction

Central Bank (henceforth, CB) communication has become increasingly important in the past 20 years for the world economy (Blinder et al., 2008). Until the mid-1990s, there was consensus that central bankers should remain more or less silent and, if urged to make official statements, should try to hide their personal believes and assessments. This code of conduct changed fundamentally in recent years. Especially in times of unconventional monetary policy, central bankers are now trying to communicate proactively to economic agents, to give forward guidance and, thereby, try to increase the effectiveness of monetary policy (Lucca and Trebbi, 2009). This has led to a fast growing economic literature about the content, type and timing of CB communications and the observable effects on the economy (e.g. Ehrmann and Fratzscher, 2007b,a).

CB communication and the reactions it causes are, in essence, verbally encoded—both in terms of official statements being issued as well as their assessment by other economic players and information gate-keepers (e.g., journalists, lobbyists). Hence, more recent empirical work tries to incorporate NLP methods into economic analyses, e.g., using topic modeling (e.g. Kawamura et al., 2019) or information theory-based scores (Lucca and Trebbi, 2009). However, these analyses are based on the assumption that statements by CBs are free from emotions and contain factual information only.

But it is quite unlikely that even experienced communicators can fully hide their emotions in such a way that they cannot be traced by analytic means. Hence, NLP methods might help reveal latent emotional loadings in CB communiqués.

Yet, if emotions can be identified, what is their added value for the interpretation of CB communication? In this paper, we intend to gather preliminary evidence that once emotional traces can be unlocked from CB communication, this additional information might help to better understand purely quantitative time series data signalling economic development congruent with emotional moves in CB press releases.

Regarding NLP, most previous work on emotion focused purely on *polarity*, a rather simplified representation of the richness of human affective states in terms of positive–negative distinctions. For example, Nopp and Hanbury (2015) deal with sentiment analysis for exploring attitudes and opinions about risk in textual disclosures issued by banks and derive sentiment scores that quantify uncertainty, negativity, and positivity in the analyzed documents (a collection of more than 500 CEO letters and outlook sections extracted from bank annual reports). The analysis of aggre-

Proceedings of the Second Workshop on Economics and Natural Language Processing, pages 16–21
Hong Kong, November 4. ©2019 Association for Computational Linguistics

gated figures revealed strong and significant correlations between uncertainty or negativity in textual disclosures and the quantitative risk indicator's future evolution.

In contrast, a growing number of researchers start focusing on more complex and informative representations of affective states, often following distinct psychological research traditions (Yu et al., 2016; Wang et al., 2016; Mohammad, 2018; Buechel and Hahn, 2018b).

Studies applying NLP methods to various other fields seem to benefit strongly from such additional information. For example, Kim et al. (2017) examine the relationship between literary genres and emotional plot development finding that, in contrast to other, more predictive emotion categories, *Joy* as a common emotional category is only moderately helpful for genre classification. More closely related to us, Bollen et al. (2011) predict stock market prices based on Twitter data. They find evidence that more complex emotion measurements allow for more accurate predictions than polarity alone. The present study provides further evidence for this general observation focusing on the well-established emotional dimensions of *Valence, Arousal, Dominance* (VAD) (Bradley and Lang, 1994) in CB statements.

To the best of our knowledge, VAD measurements have neither been applied to analyzing verbal communication in the macro-economic field, in general, nor to CB communication, in particular. We show in this paper—based on the analysis of the press statements of the U.S. Federal Reserve (Fed) and the European Central Bank (ECB)—that CB communication is anything but free from emotions. We show that particularly the dimension of *Dominance* is of high relevance and heavily depends on the state of the economy. Furthermore, communication also along the *Valence* and *Arousal* dimensions is largely affected by the individual CB presidents in office. Overall, this provides preliminary evidence that the presence of emotional loading in monetary policy communication, which is of high importance to central bankers, correlates with quantitative macro-economic indicators. Our findings provide promising avenues for further research, as the real effects of emotions on CB communication have largely been neglected in economic research.

Compared with the March 2019 ECB staff macroeconomic projections, the outlook for real GDP growth has been revised up by 0.1 percentage points for 2019 and has been revised down by 0.2 percentage points for 2020 and by 0.1 percentage points for 2021. The risks surrounding the euro area growth outlook remain tilted to the downside, on account of the prolonged presence of uncertainties, related to geopolitical factors, the rising threat of protectionism and vulnerabilities in emerging markets.

Figure 1: Excerpt of ECB statement from June 6, 2019.

2 Data

We Web-scraped the policy statements issued by the ECB and the Fed from their Web pages, starting with the first communiqué by the ECB when it formally replaced the European Monetary Institute in June 1998. The most recent documents for both ECB and Fed have been issued in June 2019. These statements contain an assessment of the economic situation by the CB, its policy decisions and the main arguments underlying them. Altogether we assembled 230 documents from the ECB and 181 from the Fed that contain on average 1583 and 417 tokens, respectively. We illustrate the particular style of these documents with an excerpt in Figure 1.

3 Methods

Measuring the emotional content of natural language utterances has become a particularly rich area of research. The choice of an adequate emotion representation format, i.e., the mathematical

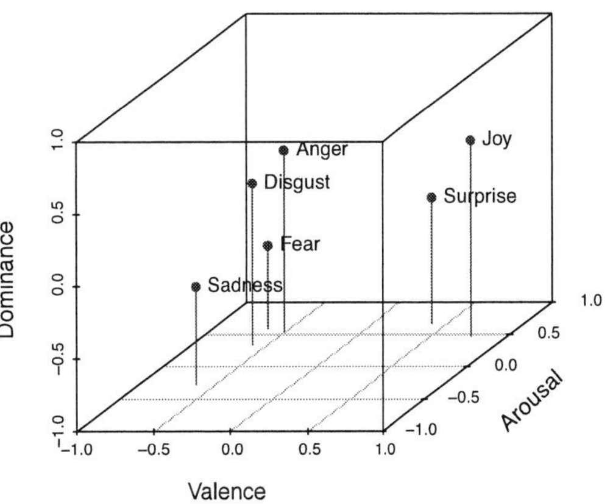

Figure 2: Affective space spanned by the Valence-Arousal-Dominance (VAD) model, together with the position of six basic emotions. Adapted from Buechel and Hahn (2016).

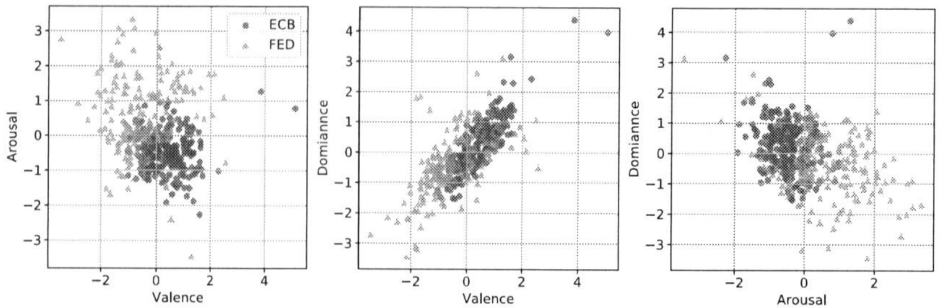

Figure 3: Scatterplot array of bivariate emotion distribution in ECB statements (blue circles) vs. Fed statements (orange triangles) with respect to *Valence* and *Arousal* (left), *Valence* and *Dominance* (center), and *Arousal* and *Dominance* (right). VAD scores are centered and scaled.

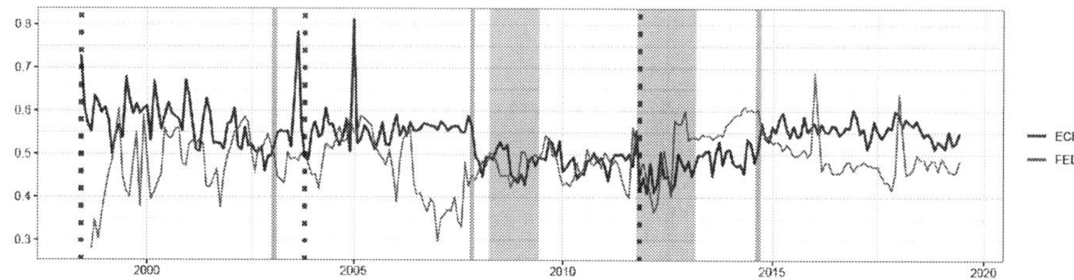

Figure 4: Dominance series for ECB (blue line) and Fed (green). Vertical dotted lines indicate beginning of ECB presidency (Duisenberg: 1998, Trichet: 2003, Draghi: 2011). Red vertical (solid) lines indicate break dates. Shaded areas highlight Euro area recession periods.

domain of the label space and its interpretation in terms of psychological theory, has become a crucial aspect of computational emotion analysis (in contrast to work focusing only on polarity) (Buechel and Hahn, 2017).

The majority of prior work follows the so-called *discrete* approach to emotion representation where a small set of universal *basic emotions* (Ekman, 1992), such as *Joy*, *Anger*, and *Sadness*, is stipulated. Equally popular in psychology though is the *dimensional* approach which represents emotions as real-valued vectors, having components such as *Valence* (pleasure vs. displeasure), *Arousal* (calmness vs. excitement) and *Dominance* (being controlled by vs. having control over a social situation; Bradley and Lang 1994). Figure 2 provides an illustration of these dimensions relative to common emotional categories. In this work, we employ the VAD format because of its greater flexibility, following our previous work (Buechel et al., 2016; Händschke et al., 2018).

Given the relatively high average token number per document in our corpus, we adopted a comparably simple lexicon-based approach which models document emotion based on word frequency combined with empirical measurements of lexical-ized word emotions.[1] Such *emotion lexicons* have a long tradition in psychology (Stone et al., 1966) and are nowadays available for various emotion formats and many different language (Buechel and Hahn, 2018a). Roughly speaking, their creation follows a questionnaire study-like design. For English VAD scores, the lexicon by Warriner et al. (2013) is a common choice due its large coverage (14k lexical units) which we adopt as well.

For the computation of document-level VAD scores, we rely on the open-source tool JEMAS Buechel and Hahn (2016)).[2] It estimates the emotion value of a document d, $\bar{e}(d)$, as weighted average of the empirical emotion values of the words in d, $e(w)$:

$$\bar{e}(d) := \frac{\sum_{w \in d} \lambda(w, d) \times e(w)}{\sum_{w \in d} \lambda(w, d)} \qquad (1)$$

where $e(w)$ is defined as the vector representing the neutral emotion, if w is not covered by the lexicon, and λ denotes some term weighting function. Here, we use absolute term frequency.

---

[1] Although less reliable for individual sentences than neural methods, lexicon-based methods still perform well on longer documents since the larger amount of word material improves predictions based on word frequency statistics (Sap et al., 2014).

[2] https://github.com/JULIELab/JEmAS

For our subsequent time series study, we process the CB corpus (see Section 2) using JEMAS. The result is one three-dimensional VAD value per document. As both an exploratory analysis and sanity check, we center and scale the resulting data and visualize them as scatterplot array (see Figure 3). ECB statements are higher in *Valence* and *Dominance* but lower in *Arousal* than Fed statements (in all cases $p < .001$; Mann–Whitney U test). As often observed (Warriner et al., 2013), *Valence* and *Dominance* have a strong linear correlation ($r = .758$).

Since neither the ECB nor the Fed hold monthly meetings, the corresponding time series of the emotion scores have missing values across the sample at a monthly frequency. A standard procedure to deal with this is linear interpolation. This appears appropriate for the ECB, since its meetings always took place at a frequent and regular pace, resulting in only 11% missing data points on a monthly basis. The Fed, however, successively increased the number of statements following their meetings. Initially, they only communicated after a policy change, but later decided to do so after each meeting. There are eight regular meetings per year plus additional sessions as required. This results in fewer data points than for the ECB, with roughly a third of data points missing.

In order to avoid artifacts due to the interpolation procedure, we alternatively apply the method of Schumacher and Breitung (2006). They use the correlation between a series affected by missing values and another, complete time series to interpolate the missing data points. The linearly interpolated series of the emotion scores are highly correlated with a broad set of economic data in their respective geographic area (see Table 1): we compiled data sets for the Euro area and the US covering a measure of the change in the real economy (approximated by industrial production), inflation, unemployment and interest rates. These

		production	inflation	unemploy.	services
ECB	V	0.32	0.19	-0.45	0.42
	A	-0.11	0.24	-0.34	-0.23
	D	0.24	-0.12	-0.32	0.53
Fed	V	0.04	-0.03	0.00	0.07
	A	0.05	0.52	-0.56	0.12
	D	-0.03	-0.17	0.10	-0.03

Table 1: VAD scores and their correlation with a broad set of economic indicators (excerpt).

are the main economic variables in most small-scale economic models. We add business and consumer survey data to incorporate forward looking elements and retail sales to complement the industry data with service sector-based information.

As one may expect, the *Valence* measurements are correlated with all activity measures, at least for the ECB. This may be due to the description of the current state of the economy inherent in the statements, which necessarily apply words with a positive or negative connotation based on the business cycle phase. Interestingly, this does not hold for the Fed, and, moreover, the *Arousal* and *Dominance* scores are also highly correlated with economic variables, particularly with inflation and unemployment—the CBs' main (direct or intermediate) target variables.

The Schumacher/Breitung procedure generates VAD-time series which, for the ECB, look virtually unchanged in comparison with the interpolated series, while the corresponding Fed scores are more volatile. For the latter reason, we stick to linear interpolation, while the results from the ECB case confirm that this method does not induce too much bias. Finally, to avoid interpolation altogether, we check whether the results persist under a qualitative perspective, if we repeat the following analysis on series aggregated to quarterly frequency.

4 Results

We perform standard break tests on the VAD scores; they are designed to detect endogenous changes in the underlying statistical process (which we model as auto-regressive, moving-average). Since Augmented-Dickey-Fuller tests indicate that these series are non-stationary, we use detrended data and find that the results also hold for the data in first differences. Focusing on the ECB, the break tests endogenously reveal three break points for each sentiment series. It has to be emphasized that the applied break tests return an endogenous break date without any restrictions by the researcher. Thus, a break date returned in proximity to a specific event makes it likely that the hypothesis of this event being causal for the break will not be rejected. A specific event study, however, is left for future research. Focusing on the ECB series, it turns out that, interestingly, independent tests for the three series reveal neighbouring break dates—either occurring around the change in presidency or key economic events (see Figure 4 for the dominance series).

The first break, in 2003, is close for the *Valence* and *Arousal* series (in July and September, respectively) and somewhat earlier for the *Dominance* series (in February). The second break is detected in winter 2008/09; again the points are close for *Valence* and *Arousal* (January '09 and September '08, respectively) and earlier for *Dominance* (in November '07, just a month before the global crisis originated in the US). The third break appears unrelated between the VAD series: it occurs in October 2011 for the *Valence* series, in February 2013 for the *Arousal* series and in September 2014 for the *Dominance* series.

This illustrates that the breakpoints, by and large, either coincide with major economic turning points, or the change in presidency of the respective CB: the first one, when Wim Duisenberg was followed by Jean-Claude Trichet in October 2003. The second break is close to the outbreak of the Great Recession, which is a common feature in most economic data due to the massive impact the global recession had on most variables. Hence, not only did the economy change drastically at that time, but also the emotions expressed by President Trichet became different. The *Dominance* series, in particular, expresses this phenomenon: With the outbreak of the crisis, the corresponding emotion scores decreased markedly and remained low until the change in presidency in fall 2011. Since Mario Draghi became ECB President this score started to recover, as evidenced by the clear uptrend; the third break point also tracks this; it occurred when the *Dominance* scores settled down on a new, higher level.

5 Conclusion

The findings of our analysis are threefold: We showed that central bankers, assumed to be among the most technically talking economic agents (for reasons of an assumed and/or desired communication efficiency), are prone to emotions which, in addition, are strongly influenced by the economic situation. The Great Recession also left its mark in the emotions of President Trichet who, according to emotion analysis coupled with standard econometric tools, switched to a markedly more submissive language. Interestingly, this attitude slowly recovered towards a more dominant stance once Mario Draghi took office. Thus, finally, our anal-

ysis shows that CB communication depends much on the person presiding it, albeit the shift to a different emotional stance, e.g. in *Dominance*, fades in only gradually.

Acknowledgments

We would like to thank the anonymous reviewers for their detailed and constructive comments.

References

Alan S Blinder, Michael Ehrmann, Marcel Fratzscher, Jakob De Haan, and David-Jan Jansen. 2008. Central bank communication and monetary policy: a survey of theory and evidence. *Journal of Economic Literature*, 46(4):910–945.

Johan Bollen, Huina Mao, and Xiaojun Zeng. 2011. TWITTER mood predicts the stock market. *Journal of Computational Science*, 2(1):1–8.

Margaret M. Bradley and Peter J. Lang. 1994. Measuring emotion: the Self-Assessment Manikin and the semantic differential. *Journal of Behavior Therapy and Experimental Psychiatry*, 25(1):49–59.

Sven Buechel and Udo Hahn. 2016. Emotion analysis as a regression problem: Dimensional models and their implications on emotion representation and metrical evaluation. In *ECAI 2016 — Proceedings of the 22nd European Conference on Artificial Intelligence. Including Prestigious Applications of Artificial Intelligence (PAIS 2016). The Hague, The Netherlands, August 29 - September 2, 2016*, number 285 in Frontiers in Artificial Intelligence and Applications, pages 1114–1122, Amsterdam, Berlin, Washington, D.C. IOS Press.

Sven Buechel and Udo Hahn. 2017. EMOBANK: studying the impact of annotation perspective and representation format on dimensional emotion analysis. In *EACL 2017 — Proceedings of the 15th Conference of the European Chapter of the Association for Computational Linguistics. Valencia, Spain, April 3-7, 2017*, volume 2: Short Papers, pages 578–585. Association for Computational Linguistics (ACL).

Sven Buechel and Udo Hahn. 2018a. Emotion representation mapping for automatic lexicon construction (mostly) performs on human level. In *COLING 2018 — Proceedings of the 27th International Conference on Computational Linguistics: Main Conference. Santa Fe, New Mexico, USA, August 20-26, 2018*, pages 2892–2904. International Committee on Computational Linguistics (ICCL).

Sven Buechel and Udo Hahn. 2018b. Word emotion induction for multiple languages as a deep multitask learning problem. In *NAACL-HLT 2018 — Proceedings of the 2018 Conference of the North American Chapter of the Association for Computational

Linguistics: Human Language Technologies, volume 1, long papers, pages 1907–1918, New Orleans, Louisiana, USA, June 1–6, 2018.

Sven Buechel, Udo Hahn, Jan Goldenstein, Sebastian G. M. Händschke, and Peter Walgenbach. 2016. Do enterprises have emotions? In *WASSA 2016 — Proceedings of the 7th Workshop on Computational Approaches to Subjectivity, Sentiment and Social Media Analysis @ NAACL-HLT 2016. San Diego, California, USA, June 16, 2016*, pages 147–153.

Michael Ehrmann and Marcel Fratzscher. 2007a. Communication by central bank committee members: different strategies, same effectiveness? *Journal of Money, Credit and Banking*, 39(2-3):509–541.

Michael Ehrmann and Marcel Fratzscher. 2007b. The timing of central bank communication. *European Journal of Political Economy*, 23(1):124–145.

Paul Ekman. 1992. An argument for basic emotions. *Cognition & Emotion*, 6(3-4):169–200.

Sebastian G. M. Händschke, Sven Buechel, Jan Goldenstein, Philipp Poschmann, Tinghui Duan, Peter Walgenbach, and Udo Hahn. 2018. A corpus of corporate annual and social responsibility reports: 280 million tokens of balanced organizational writing. In *ECONLP 2018 — Proceedings of the 1st Workshop on Economics and Natural Language Processing @ ACL 2018. Melbourne, Victoria, Australia, July 20, 2018*, pages 20–31, Stroudsburg/PA. Association for Computational Linguistics (ACL).

Kohei Kawamura, Yohei Kobashi, Masato Shizume, and Kozo Ueda. 2019. Strategic central bank communication: discourse analysis of the Bank of Japan's monthly report. *Journal of Economic Dynamics and Control*, 100:230–250.

Evgeny Kim, Sebastian Padó, and Roman Klinger. 2017. Investigating the relationship between literary genres and emotional plot development. In *LaTeCH-CLfL 2017 — Proceedings of the 1st Joint SIGHUM Workshop on Computational Linguistics for Cultural Heritage, Social Sciences, Humanities and Literature @ ACL 2017. Vancouver, British Columbia, Canada, August 4, 2017*, pages 17–26. Association for Computational Linguistics (ACL).

David O. Lucca and Francesco Trebbi. 2009. Measuring central bank communication: an automated approach with application to FOMC statements. Technical Report Working Paper No. 15367, National Bureau of Economic Research (NBER), Cambridge, MA, USA.

Saif M. Mohammad. 2018. Obtaining reliable human ratings of valence, arousal, and dominance for 20,000 english words. In *ACL 2018 — Proceedings of the 56th Annual Meeting of the Association for Computational Linguistics. Melbourne, Victoria, Australia, July 15-20, 2018*, volume 1: Long Papers, pages 174–184.

Clemens Nopp and Allan Hanbury. 2015. Detecting risks in the banking system by sentiment analysis. In *EMNLP 2015 — Proceedings of the 2015 Conference on Empirical Methods in Natural Language Processing. Lisbon, Portugal, 17-21 September 2015*, pages 591–600, Red Hook/NY. Association for Computational Linguistics (ACL), Curran Associates, Inc.

Maarten Sap, Gregory J. Park, Johannes C. Eichstaedt, Margaret L. Kern, David J. Stillwell, Michal Kosinski, Lyle H. Ungar, and Hansen Andrew Schwartz. 2014. Developing age and gender predictive lexica over social media. In *EMNLP 2014 — Proceedings of the 2014 Conference on Empirical Methods in Natural Language Processing. Doha, Qatar, October 25-29, 2014*, pages 1146–1151. Association for Computational Linguistics (ACL).

Christian Schumacher and Jörg Breitung. 2006. Real-time forecasting of GDP based on a large factor model with monthly and quarterly data. Discussion Paper Series 1: Economic Studies 2006/33, Deutsche Bundesbank.

Philip J Stone, Dexter C Dunphy, and Marshall S Smith. 1966. *The General Inquirer: A Computer Approach to Content Analysis*. MIT Press.

Jin Wang, Liang-Chih Yu, K. Robert Lai, and Xuejie Zhang. 2016. Dimensional sentiment analysis using a regional CNN-LSTM model. In *ACL 2016 — Proceedings of the 54th Annual Meeting of the Association for Computational Linguistics. Berlin, Germany, August 7-12, 2016*, volume 2: Short Papers, pages 225–230, Stroudsburg, PA. Association for Computational Linguistics (ACL).

Amy Beth Warriner, Victor Kuperman, and Marc Brysbaert. 2013. Norms of valence, arousal, and dominance for 13,915 English lemmas. *Behavior Research Methods*, 45(4):1191–1207.

Liang-Chih Yu, Lung-Hao Lee, Shuai Hao, Jin Wang, Yunchao He, Jun Hu, K. Robert Lai, and Xuejie Zhang. 2016. Building Chinese affective resources in valence-arousal dimensions. In *NAACL-HLT 2016 — Proceedings of the 2016 Conference of the North American Chapter of the Association for Computational Linguistics: Human Language Technologies. San Diego, California, USA, June 12-17, 2016*, pages 540–545, Stroudsburg/PA. Association for Computational Linguistics (ACL).

Forecasting Firm Material Event Sequences from 8-K Reports

Shuang Zhai
Iowa State University
szhai@iastate.edu

Zhu Zhang
Iowa State University
zhuzhang@iastate.edu

Abstract

In this paper, we show deep learning models can be used to forecast firm material event sequences based on the contents in the company's 8-K Current Reports. Specifically, we exploit state-of-the-art neural architectures, including sequence-to-sequence (Seq2Seq) architecture and attention mechanisms, in the model. Our 8K-powered deep learning model demonstrates promising performance in forecasting firm future event sequences. The model is poised to benefit various stakeholders, including management and investors, by facilitating risk management and decision making.

1   Introduction

One Corporate Event Sequence (CES) is a sequence of events that take place at one company during a period of time. A series of company events can represent corporate strategy and future plans. Therefore, CES can be used as a tool to probe corporate strategy and decision-making behaviors.

Investors can use existing CES to project a company's future CES. For instance, an acquisition is a sign for financing, and insufficient funding is a vane for refinancing. Similarly, a failing operational decision can bring an executive personnel change, and a new senior-level appointment can be expected after that. Since CES embodies consistency (to corporate strategy) and continuity (to time), it is equipped to illuminate a maze pathway for organizational strategy evaluation.

Researches increasingly reveal the merit of textual data in financial studies. Many studies are centered on the financial market, such as a firm's stock price, return, and volatility (Fang and Peress, 2009; Tetlock, 2010; Edmans, 2011). Meanwhile, the high dimensionality characteristic of textual data presents challenges to traditional econometric models. Therefore, they render themselves to machine learning and deep learning models naturally. Deep learning models have become gradually popular in finance applications recently, and many of them have focused on market-related tasks as well (Ding et al., 2014, 2015). These models, however, didn't take corporate strategy into account and didn't focus on the sequence nature of corporate events.

U.S. Security and Exchange Commission (SEC) requires the publicly-traded company to file Form 8-K (also called 'Material Event Report' or 'Current Report') when certain types of the corporate event take place. In general, an 8-K report should be filed when the company has an event that its shareholders should be aware of. A material event is defined as *a matter if there is a substantial likelihood that a reasonable person would consider it important* [1], and a "rule of thumb" impact scale of a material event is *five to ten percent of net income* [2].

Although public companies are also required to file Form 10-K (annual report), and Form 10-Q (quarterly report), 10-K/Qs have apparent and significant drawbacks compared to 8-Ks. 10-K/Qs are designed to cover a mixed category of information. It is easy for them to plunge lower readability and create higher barrier for amateur readers. While the length of 10-K/Qs gets longer and longer (Cazier and Pfeiffer, 2015), not all investors have the skill to decipher the insightful message from the lengthy 10-K/Qs. When they encounter difficulties in 10K/Qs, most retail investors do not have enough resources as advanced institutional investors do. Most importantly, 10-K/Qs are re-

---

[1] https://www.sec.gov/interps/account/sab99.htm
[2] Financial Accounting Standards Board ("FASB"), Statement of Financial Accounting Concepts No. 2, Qualitative Characteristics of Accounting Information ("Concepts Statement No. 2"), Concepts Statement No. 2, 167.

Proceedings of the Second Workshop on Economics and Natural Language Processing, pages 22–30
Hong Kong, November 4. ©2019 Association for Computational Linguistics

leased long time after the event and get considerably prolonged-release intervals. It means investors have to wait one quarter or longer to see the updated official release from the company.

Various stakeholders, not only investors but also management teams and regulators, can find CES useful. CES provides not only corporate strategy hints but also corporate operation patterns. Given the continuous characteristic of CES, it notches up contents for stakeholders to achieve higher profits and a better position in a timely manner.

Given the versatile benefits of 8Ks and the textual data forecasting ability of deep learning models, we propose an end-to-end sequence-to-sequence neural network to predict corporate event sequences from 8-K reports in this paper.

2 Related Techniques

2.1 Gated Recurrent Units (GRUs)

Gated Recurrent Unit (GRU) is a representative deep learning architecture, and it was first proposed by Cho et al. (2014). Numerous works have been done in natural language processing using GRUs, such as part of speech (POS) tagging, information extraction, syntactic parsing, speech recognition, machine translation (Cho et al., 2014), and question answering.

2.2 Sequence to Sequence (Seq2Seq) Neural Network

Sequence-to-sequence (seq2seq) model was introduced by Sutskever et al. (2014). It is widely used by machine translation tasks (Bahdanau et al., 2015; Luong et al., 2015), i.e. translating sentences from one language to another language, such as French to English. Attention mechanism has been explored broadly in recent publications. The intuition for attention technique in natural language processing is to assign higher attention to texts where contain more information for the task on hand. Yang et al. (2016) employed both word-level and sentence-level attentions for document classification task. Wang et al. (2016) proposed an aspect-level attention to capture different sentiments for different aspects in a sentence. Ma et al. (2017) proposed an interactive attention architecture that models the interaction between the context and target for sentiment classification task. More recently, Vaswani et al. (2017) used multi-head attentions alone to solve sequence prediction problems which are traditionally handled by other neural network techniques such as Long Short-Term Memory and Convolution Neural Networks. We are inspired by Bahdanau et al. (2015), Luong et al. (2015), Kadlec et al. (2016) and Cui et al. (2017) to compute event attention for our prediction task.

3 Material Events and Form 8-K Current Reports

3.1 Related Works

Various items [3] are required to be filed in company 8-K reports. Many studies have tried to categorize 8-Ks into different categories. Zhao (2016) classified 8-Ks into seven categories: 1) information about business and operations (OPR), 2) financial information (FIN), 3) matters related to the exchange or trading of the securities, 4) information related to financial accountants and financial statements, 5) corporate governance and management (GOV), 6) events related to Regulation Fair Disclosure (REG), 7) other events considered important to the firm (OTH). OPR, FIN, GOV, REG, and OTH are the five major 8-K categories which cover more than 95% of all 8-K reports in their study.

Feuerriegel and Pröllochs (2018) used Latent Dirichlet Allocation (LDA) method and categorized 8-K reports into topics: energy sector, insurance sector, change of trustee, real estate, corporate structure, loan payment, amendment of shareholder rights, earnings results, securities sales, stock option award, credit rating, income statements, business strategy, securities lending, management change, health care sector, tax report, stock dilution, mergers and acquisitions, and public relations. Earnings results and public relations are the top two topics in their study. He and Plumlee (2019) categorized voluntary items (Item 2.02, 7.01, and 8.01) into a business combination, conference presentations, dividend announcement, litigation, patents, restructuring, security offerings, share repurchase, and shareholder agreement.

3.2 Our Approach

However, none of the above studies tried to categorize 8-Ks by the event nature. Meanwhile, certain items are mandatory to be reported and other items are voluntary. Therefore, we first read

---

[3]https://www.sec.gov/fast-answers/answersform8khtm.html

thousands of 8-Ks by ourselves and designed taxonomies to holistically characterize 8-Ks into multiple event types, based on human understanding of the report content and nature of the event. Then, we map every report to one of our event types for analysis. We list our event types in Table 1, and they are our prediction's *target variables*. Since some reports can be filed under different item numbers (from 1.01 to 8.01, we eliminated 9.01 Exhibits), the mapping between Report Items and Event Types is many to many. In other words, one report item number can also be seen in different event types. The bold item numbers in Table 1 are items shown in more than one event types. For instance, senior personnel change can be filed under Item 5.02 Departure of Directors or Certain Officers; Election of Directors; Appointment of Certain Officers; Compensatory Arrangements of Certain Officers, or Item 8.01 Other Events.

4 Problem Definition

4.1 Background

The goal of our work is to predict firm's future event sequences, based on its historical event sequences. Therefore, our prediction task is to solve a sequence-to-sequence problem. In particular, we use corporate event sequences in memory M to predict event sequences in forecasting horizon H. Historical event sequences are collected from corporate 8-K reports, and all events are identified by event types listed in Table 1. Memory M and forecasting horizon H are formed by smaller time intervals j and q, respectively. The time structure of our model is illustrated in Figure 1.

4.2 A Real-world Example

We can also view the sequence-to-sequence prediction as a story completion task. Particularly, once we know what events happened in the past, we can predict what events are likely to occur in the future, to complete the story. We present an example of corporate events sequence in Figure 2 to demonstrate the real-world practice and the importance of the problem.

Figure 2 shows an example of the company AT&T event sequence during time t-M to t+H, and it illustrates how the historical corporate events during time t-M to t can forecast and impact future corporate events during time t to t+H. For example, at time t-M, AT&T wins several wireless spectrum auctions from the Federal Communica-

tions Commission (FCC). Because of the auction win, AT&T needs more capital to support the new business. Therefore, we see AT&T has arranged loans and reported them in its 8-K afterward. In another stream, similar to its competitors, AT&T also desires to tap into the content industry. It announces the acquisition of Time Warner to support this corporate blueprint. As we have learned previously, because of the acquisition, AT&T needs more money to finance this deal. As a result, AT&T has filed a loan financing activity in its following 8-K report. Meanwhile, possibly because of the corporate strategy disagreement, AT&T's business solution CEO, who was a supporter of expanding business in hardware instead of the content industry, announces retirement. Given what we have learned so far, we can foresee that several corporate events can have higher chances to become real in the future. For instance, if the previous financing amounts were not enough for the Time Warner acquisition, AT&T have to require more loans. We can observe the loan financing activity admittedly happened in the forecasting horizon. Moreover, because of the acquisition, AT&T would need to make arrangements for Time Warner's executive members, which indeed happened in the forecasting window. AT&T announced Time Warner's CEO duty after the acquisition was completed. Additionally, after the acquisition was completed, AT&T has realized additional financial needs for the combined business. Therefore, we notice AT&T reported another loan activity after the completion of the acquisition. This example tells us that historical corporate events can affect not only *what* type of event will happen in the future, but also *when* the event will occur in the future.

4.3 Formal Definition

Let's formally define the problem as,

$$E_{(i)j} = g_{k=0}^{|K|}(S_{(i)jk}) \tag{1}$$

$$y_{(i)q} = f_{j=0}^{M}(E_{(i)j}) \tag{2}$$

$$y_{(i)q} \in Y_{(i)}^{H} \tag{3}$$

where,

- y denotes the event types in Table 1, Y^H denotes the event sequence during H, and sequence $Y^H = [y_1, ..., y_H]$.

ID	Event Type	Code	Report Item	Examples
1	Business combination and restructuring	BC	**1.01, 1.02**, 2.01, **7.01, 8.01**	merger, acquisition, join venture, separation, spin-off
2	Financial activities	FN	**1.01, 1.02**, 2.03, 2.04, 2.05, 2.06, 3.02, 6.01, 6.02, 6.03, 6.04, 6.05, **7.01, 8.01**	lend, borrow, loan, Notes, payment, debt, stock, repurchase, dividend, asset-backed securiteis (ABS)
3	Operation activities	OA	**1.01, 1.02, 7.01, 8.01**	operation, contract, consulting, service, product, supply
4	Senior personnel change	PC	**1.01, 1.02**, 5.02, **7.01, 8.01**	executive officer/director, retire, leave, appointment
5	Information disclosure	ID	2.02, 4.01, 4.02, 5.07, 5.08, **7.01, 8.01**	conference, presentation, statement, exhibit
6	Document update	DU	3.03, 5.01, 5.03, 5.05, 5.06, **7.01, 8.01**	by-laws, code of ethics
7	Intellectual property activities	IP	**1.01, 1.02, 7.01, 8.01**	intellectual property, patent approval
8	Litigation and lawsuit	LL	**1.01, 1.02, 7.01, 8.01**	settlement, litigation, lawsuit
9	Delisting, trading suspension	DL	3.01, 5.04, **7.01, 8.01**	delisting, trading suspension
10	Bankruptcy	BK	1.03, **7.01, 8.01**	bankruptcy

Table 1: Event Types (*target variables*)

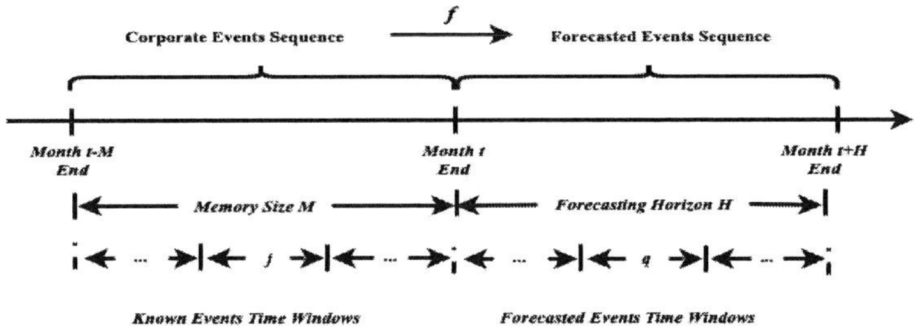

Figure 1: Time structure of the model

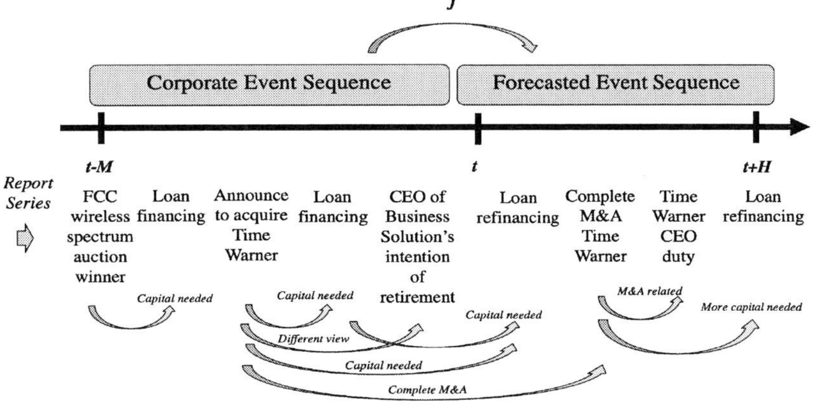

Figure 2: Corporate event sequence forecasting example: AT&T

- M denotes the size of memory, and H denotes the size of forecasting horizon, both are measured in terms of the number of time windows.

- i indexes companies.

- j indexes time window in M, and $j = \{1, ..., M\}$.

- q indexes time window in H, and $q = \{1, ..., H\}$.

- ev denotes event index, and $|Ev|$ denotes the total number of event types.

- $|K|$ denotes the total number of events per time window.

- $S_{(i)jk}$ is the embedding of the kth event of company C_i in time window j, and $E_{(i)j}$ is the aggregate event embedding of company C_i in time window j.

- g is a function that aggregates multiple event embeddings into one embedding.

- f is a learned model (function) that maps all event embeddings in memory to forecasting horizon.

In principle, g and f can be parameterized as any function approximator.

5 Model

5.1 GRU model

Since our task works on time sequences and is formed as a sequence-to-sequence (seq2seq) problem, we use *GRU* as the backbone of our model. Additionally, we use *encoder-decoder* framework as the architecture in our model.

In the encoder of the model, we train our event type embeddings in the *Event Embedding Layer*. Multiple reports can be filed at the same time window. Therefore, at each time window, we select the top $|K|$ event embeddings for each company, based on each event embedding's L2 norm value. We institute various treatments of function g in Equation 1, such as attention mechanism. In the *Event Attention Layer*, we implement attention to the top $|K|$ event embeddings and obtain the weighted embedding at each time window.

We define our *Event Attention Layer* as,

$$\widetilde{h}_{(i)j} = sigmoid(W_{(i)jk}S_{(i)jk} + b_{(i)j}) \quad (4)$$

$$\alpha_{(i)jk} = softmax(W_{(i)j}\widetilde{h}_{(i)j}) \quad (5)$$

$$E_{(i)j} = \sum_{k=1}^{|K|} \alpha_{(i)jk}S_{(i)jk} \quad (6)$$

The weighted sum context vector $E_{(i)j}$ is used as the aggregated semantic representation of the company events at each time window. Next, $E_{(i)j}$ is fed into the following *Event Embedding Layer*.

In the vanilla GRU model, the last hidden state of the encoder is directly connected to the decoder. At every time t in the decoder, the hidden state hs_t is used to predict the current timestamp event type in the *Prediction Layer*, and we use $softmax$ function to compute y_t as,

$$y_t = softmax(W_{st}hs_t) \quad (7)$$

5.2 GRU_attention model

We implement the *Alignment Attention Layer* in the GRU_attention model.

In the *encoder-decoder* framework, information from the encoder is carried over to the decoder. To be able to capture what events happened in history play more roles in the prediction horizon, we employ attention mechanism (Bahdanau et al., 2015; Luong et al., 2015; Kadlec et al., 2016; Cui et al., 2017) to capture the dynamics. The GRU_attention model's decoder looks at every hidden state in the encoder. The *Alignment Attention Layer* aligns different attention values to hidden states in the encoder, and aggregates them. We follow the "general" approach in Luong et al. (2015) and obtain attention scores between the target sequence and the input sequence as,

$$score(h_{tr}, h_{sr}) = h_{tr}^{T}W_a h_{sr} \quad (8)$$

, where h_{tr} is the hidden state of target sequence and h_{sr} is the hidden state of the source sequence.

The context vector c_t is the weighted sum of the product of attention scores and the hidden states in the encoder.

$$c_t = \sum_{j=0}^{M} score(h_{tr}, h_{sr})_j h_{sr_j} \quad (9)$$

$$hs_t = tanh(W_c[c_t; h_{tr}]) \quad (10)$$

, where $[.;.]$ denotes concatenation along the sequence dimension.

We illustrate the GRU_attention model in Figure 3.

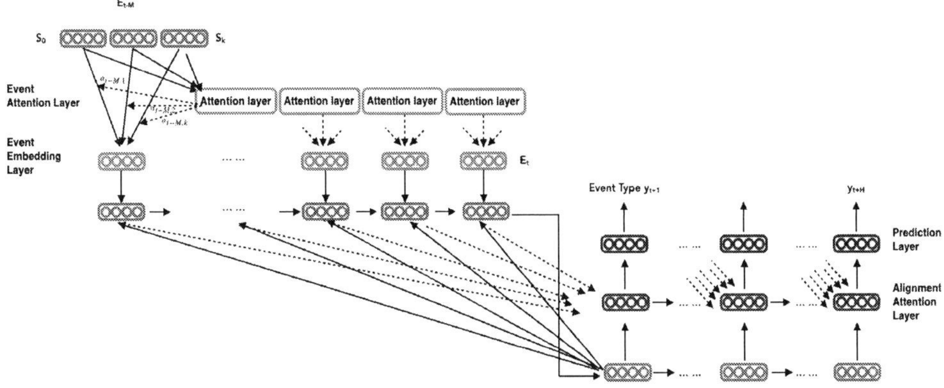

Figure 3: Corporate Event Sequence Forecasting: GRU_attention Model

6 Experiments

6.1 Evaluation Models

We evaluate the following models in our experiments:

- **MCMC_baseline**: Markov Chain Monte Carlo (MCMC) simulation. (Details are discussed in 6.2.)

- **GRU**: event sequence as input and without attention.

- **GRU_attention**: event sequence as input and with attention.

6.2 MCMC baseline

For every company, we gathered its event sequences during the entire experimental period, and constructed an event transition matrix.

Given the obtained transition matrix, we can implement the Markov Chain Monte Carlo (MCMC) simulations. In particular, we view each row of the transition matrix as each event type's probability distribution. We recognize every event type at the last training timestamp as the current event type E_t, then we can draw the next event type E_{t+1} given E_t's probability distribution. By doing this step repetitively, we can sample E_{t+2} based on E_{t+1}'s probability distribution, and so on. Finally, we reach E_{t+H} and complete the sampling process. In the experiment, for each event type E_t, we sample its sequences 100 times, and we use the averaged sequence performance as our model baseline.

6.3 Per Event Type Evaluation

We experiment a threshold to convert the $softmax$ result of each event type at time t into binary format as,

$$Eval_{ev,t} = \begin{cases} 1 & if\, y_{ev,t} > threshold \\ 0 & otherwise \end{cases}$$

In experiments, we set the threshold value as 0.1. We evaluate classification performance per event type. In particular, we compute classification criteria, i.e., precision, recall, and F1 score, for each event type and evaluate our model results.

In addition, since predicting event type correctly within a reasonable temporal approximate period is also important in real business setting, we use two approaches, i.e. *precise evaluation* and *fuzzy evaluation* to evaluate our models.

For each event type, we compute its true positive (TP), false positive (FP), false positive (FP), and true negative (TN), and evaluate the model's precision (Pr), recall (Re), and F-measure (F1) accordingly.

Precise evaluation: we compute the confusion matrix at the precise time t as,

$$Precision_{ev,t}(Pr_{ev,t}) = \frac{TP_{ev,t}}{TP_{ev,t} + FP_{ev,t}} \quad (11)$$

$$Recall_{ev,t}(Re_{ev,t}) = \frac{TP_{ev,t}}{TP_{ev,t} + FN_{ev,t}} \quad (12)$$

$$F1_{ev,t} = \frac{2 * Pr_{ev,t} * Re_t}{Pr_{ev,t} + Re_{ev,t}} \quad (13)$$

Fuzzy evaluation: because correctly predicting event type that close to the exact time t also has practical implications, i.e., forecasting accurately of the event type close to time t is also useful in reality, we compute the confusion matrix within $[t - z, t + z]$ time window, and $z \in [1, 2, ...]$. We update the true positive for precision and recall for $t \in [t - z, t + z]$, and re-compute the precision, recall, and F1 measures for $t \in [t - z, t + z]$ as,

$$Pr_{ev,[t-z,t+z]} = \frac{TP_{ev,[t-z,t+z]}}{TP_{ev,[t-z,t+z]} + FP_{ev,t}} \quad (14)$$

$$Re_{ev,[t-z,t+z]} = \frac{TP_{ev,[t-z,t+z]}}{TP_{ev,[t-z,t+z]} + FN_{ev,t}} \quad (15)$$

$$F1_{ev,[t-z,t+z]} = \frac{2 * Pr_{ev,[t-z,t+z]} * Re_{ev,[t-z,t+z]}}{Pr_{ev,[t-z,t+z]} + Re_{ev,[t-z,t+z]}} \quad (16)$$

Precise evaluation is a special case of fuzzy evaluation when $z=0$. We report both precision evaluation and fuzzy evaluation $z=1$ results in the result section.

6.4 Data

We use 8-K Current Reports filed to SEC's EDGAR system *(the Electronic Data Gathering, Analysis, and Retrieval system)* between August of the year 2004 and December of the year 2018 as our data. Our study focuses on the Fortune 1,000 companies, and we use them as our focal companies.

Given the time constraint, we only use 200 companies data in the training set, 45 companies data in the validation set, and 45 companies data in the testing set. We split the dataset by company. In the end, we had 8,400 sequences in training, 2,304 sequences in validation, and 2,090 sequences in testing.

6.5 Preprocessing

We extracted the company name, report content, and published date from each 8-K report in *EDGAR*. We use Python for reports downloading and content extraction. We use Spacy [4] fuzzy matching to map report content to event types in Table 1.

6.6 Model Training

We train event embeddings in our model. In the experiments, we define time window i to be a month and memory size $M = 36$. We define time window q to be a month and the forecasting horizon $H = 12$. Given the event reporting nature, we

---

[4]https://spacy.io/.

use $|K| = 2$ in our experiments. We use $softmax$ (Goodfellow et al., 2016) as the activation function, Adam (Kingma and Ba, 2014) as the optimizer, and Cross Entropy (CE) as the loss function.

7 Discussion

We show our precise model performance in Table 2, fuzzy model performance in Table 3, and model perplexity in Table 4.

First of all, the model performance tells us the potential to predict firm event sequences using a sequence-to-sequence neural network. The performance tables show the direction of designing the corporate event sequence prediction problem as a story completion task is promising, although there are rooms to keep improving the model.

At the same time, one thing we want to point out is the dataset is unbalanced by following business nature. In other words, some event types happen less frequently than others. For instance, intellectual property activities, litigation and lawsuit, delisting, and bankruptcy happen much less frequently than financial activities, senior personnel change, and information disclosure. Therefore, some event types didn't generate prediction results as high as other types.

From the model results, we can see (1) the proposed sequence-to-sequence neural network models perform better than the baseline simulation model, and (2) the attention mechanism is useful on certain event type predictions as well. They both demonstrate the promising direction of the proposed problem formulation.

In both Table 2 and Table 3, we can see the sequence-to-sequence models perform better than the baseline simulation model. Moreover, when attention mechanism is added, the with attention model gains prediction performance for event types including senior personnel change, information disclosure, document updates, intellectual property activities, and delisting, in precise evaluation. The with attention model shows better performance results for business combination and restructuring, document updates, intellectual property activities, litigation and lawsuit, delisting and bankruptcy event types, in fuzzy evaluation. They show the value of the model formulation. Meanwhile, when we compare models between with attention and without attention, we can identify the usefulness of the attention mechanism on certain

Event Type	MCMC Baseline	GRU	GRU_attention
business combination and restructuring	9.68%	**19.80%**	16.42%
financial activities	20.16%	**39.01%**	36.67%
operation activities	1.78%	**4.20%**	3.40%
senior personnel change	20.52%	30.79%	**31.71%**
information disclosure	33.34%	44.41%	**46.26%**
document updates	4.22%	6.32%	**7.90%**
intellectual property activities	0.54%	0.97%	**1.01%**
litigation and lawsuit	1.13%	**1.94%**	1.78%
delisting	0.44%	0.33%	**0.62%**
bankruptcy	0.03%	**0.15%**	0.14%

Table 2: Model performance (precise evaluation, F1%)

Event Type	MCMC Baseline	GRU	GRU_attention
business combination and restructuring	22.12%	35.59%	**37.34%**
financial activities	42.27%	**62.03%**	51.33%
operation activities	3.88%	**9.28%**	9.23%
senior personnel change	42.71%	**56.96%**	51.42%
information disclosure	58.49%	**70.37%**	59.65%
document updates	9.56%	19.66%	**19.93%**
intellectual property activities	1.43%	3.03%	**3.38%**
litigation and lawsuit	2.74%	4.69%	**4.96%**
delisting	1.58%	1.66%	**2.20%**
bankruptcy	0.05%	0.30%	**0.34%**

Table 3: Model performance (fuzzy evaluation, F1%)

Event Type	MCMC Baseline	GRU	GRU_attention
Perplexity	175.28	**33.15**	33.32

Table 4: Model Perplexity

event types. Perplexity results in Table 4 also verifies the promising model design direction as well.

In a real business setting, there are other data streams can also participate in the decision making process, such as company fundamental values. We are working on the integration of multiple data streams as well.

8 Conclusion and Future Work

In this paper, we proposed sequence-to-sequence (Seq2Seq) models to forecast firm material event sequences, based on firm historical event sequences. The proposed deep learning model demonstrates promising performance and design rationale for the task of predicting firm future event sequences.

However, there are still rooms to improve our models in the future. We plan to incorporate other data streams and other techniques, such as variational autoencoder (VAE) (Kingma and Welling, 2013), Transformer (Vaswani et al., 2017) and/or BERT (Devlin et al., 2018), in the model architecture. We also plan to further investigate the economic implications of our formulation and solution.

References

Dzmitry Bahdanau, Kyunghyun Cho, and Yoshua Bengio. 2015. Neural machine translation by jointly learning to align and translate. *CoRR*, abs/1409.0473.

Richard A Cazier and Ray J Pfeiffer. 2015. Why are 10-k filings so long? *Accounting Horizons*, 30(1):1–21.

Kyunghyun Cho, Bart Van Merriënboer, Caglar Gulcehre, Dzmitry Bahdanau, Fethi Bougares, Holger Schwenk, and Yoshua Bengio. 2014. Learning phrase representations using rnn encoder-decoder for statistical machine translation. *arXiv preprint arXiv:1406.1078*.

Yiming Cui, Zhipeng Chen, Si Wei, Shijin Wang, Ting Liu, and Guoping Hu. 2017. Attention-over-attention neural networks for reading comprehension. In *Proceedings of the 55th Annual Meeting of the Association for Computational Linguistics (Volume 1: Long Papers)*, pages 593–602. Association for Computational Linguistics.

Jacob Devlin, Ming-Wei Chang, Kenton Lee, and Kristina Toutanova. 2018. Bert: Pre-training of deep bidirectional transformers for language understanding. *arXiv preprint arXiv:1810.04805*.

Xiao Ding, Yue Zhang, Ting Liu, and Junwen Duan. 2014. Using structured events to predict stock price movement: An empirical investigation. In *Proceedings of the 2014 Conference on Empirical Methods in Natural Language Processing (EMNLP)*, pages 1415–1425.

Xiao Ding, Yue Zhang, Ting Liu, and Junwen Duan. 2015. Deep learning for event-driven stock prediction. In *the 24th International Joint Conference on Artificial Intelligence*, pages 2327–2333.

Alex Edmans. 2011. Does the stock market fully value intangibles? employee satisfaction and equity prices. *Journal of Financial economics*, 101(3):621–640.

Lily Fang and Joel Peress. 2009. Media coverage and the cross-section of stock returns. *The Journal of Finance*, 64(5):2023–2052.

Stefan Feuerriegel and Nicolas Pröllochs. 2018. Investor reaction to financial disclosures across topics: An application of latent dirichlet allocation. *Decision Sciences*.

Ian Goodfellow, Yoshua Bengio, and Aaron Courville. 2016. *Deep learning*. MIT press.

Jing He and A. Marlene Plumlee. 2019. Measuring disclosure using 8k filings. *SSRN*.

Rudolf Kadlec, Martin Schmid, Ondřej Bajgar, and Jan Kleindienst. 2016. Text understanding with the attention sum reader network. In *Proceedings of the 54th Annual Meeting of the Association for Computational Linguistics (Volume 1: Long Papers)*, pages 908–918. Association for Computational Linguistics.

Diederik P Kingma and Jimmy Ba. 2014. Adam: A method for stochastic optimization. *arXiv preprint arXiv:1412.6980*.

Diederik P Kingma and Max Welling. 2013. Auto-encoding variational bayes. *arXiv preprint arXiv:1312.6114*.

Minh-Thang Luong, Hieu Pham, and Christopher D Manning. 2015. Effective approaches to attention-based neural machine translation. *arXiv preprint arXiv:1508.04025*.

Dehong Ma, Sujian Li, Xiaodong Zhang, and Houfeng Wang. 2017. Interactive attention networks for aspect-level sentiment classification. *arXiv preprint arXiv:1709.00893*.

Ilya Sutskever, Oriol Vinyals, and Quoc V Le. 2014. Sequence to sequence learning with neural networks. In *Advances in neural information processing systems*, pages 3104–3112.

Paul C Tetlock. 2010. Does public financial news resolve asymmetric information? *The Review of Financial Studies*, 23(9):3520–3557.

Ashish Vaswani, Noam Shazeer, Niki Parmar, Jakob Uszkoreit, Llion Jones, Aidan N Gomez, Łukasz Kaiser, and Illia Polosukhin. 2017. Attention is all you need. In *Advances in Neural Information Processing Systems*, pages 5998–6008.

Yequan Wang, Minlie Huang, Li Zhao, et al. 2016. Attention-based lstm for aspect-level sentiment classification. In *Proceedings of the 2016 conference on empirical methods in natural language processing*, pages 606–615.

Zichao Yang, Diyi Yang, Chris Dyer, Xiaodong He, Alex Smola, and Eduard Hovy. 2016. Hierarchical attention networks for document classification. In *Proceedings of the 2016 Conference of the North American Chapter of the Association for Computational Linguistics: Human Language Technologies*, pages 1480–1489.

Xiaofei Zhao. 2016. Does information intensity matter for stock returns? evidence from form 8-k filings. *Management Science*, 63(5):1382–1404.

Incorporating Fine-grained Events in Stock Movement Prediction

Deli Chen[1]*, Yanyan Zou[2], Keiko Harimoto[3], Ruihan Bao[3], Xuancheng Ren[1], Xu Sun[1]

[1]MOE Key Lab of Computational Linguistics, School of EECS, Peking University
[2]StatNLP Research Group, Singapore University of Technology and Design
[3]Mizuho Securities Co., Ltd.
{chendeli,renxc,xusun}@pku.edu.cn, yanyan_zou@mymail.sutd.edu.sg,
{keiko.harimoto,ruihan.bao}@mizuho-sc.com

Abstract

Considering event structure information has proven helpful in text-based stock movement prediction. However, existing works mainly adopt the coarse-grained events, which loses the specific semantic information of diverse event types. In this work, we propose to incorporate the fine-grained events in stock movement prediction. Firstly, we propose a professional finance event dictionary built by domain experts and use it to extract fine-grained events automatically from finance news. Then we design a neural model to combine finance news with fine-grained event structure and stock trade data to predict the stock movement. Besides, in order to improve the generalizability of the proposed method, we design an advanced model that uses the extracted fine-grained events as the distant supervised label to train a multi-task framework of event extraction and stock prediction. The experimental results show that our method outperforms all the baselines and has good generalizability.

1 Introduction

Stock movement plays an important role in economic activities, so the prediction of stock movement has caught a lot of attention of researchers. In recent years, employing the stock related text (such as finance news or tweets) has become the mainstream (Si et al., 2014; Ding et al., 2015; Li et al., 2015; Alostad and Davulcu, 2017; Zhong et al., 2017; Zhang et al., 2018a) of stock movement prediction task. In these text-based stock prediction works, various methods are proposed to extract semantic information from stock related text to help the prediction of stock movement. There are mainly two methods of applying text: employing raw text (Hu et al., 2018; Xu and Cohen, 2018) or coarse-grained <S,P,O> structure (subject, predicate and object) extracted from

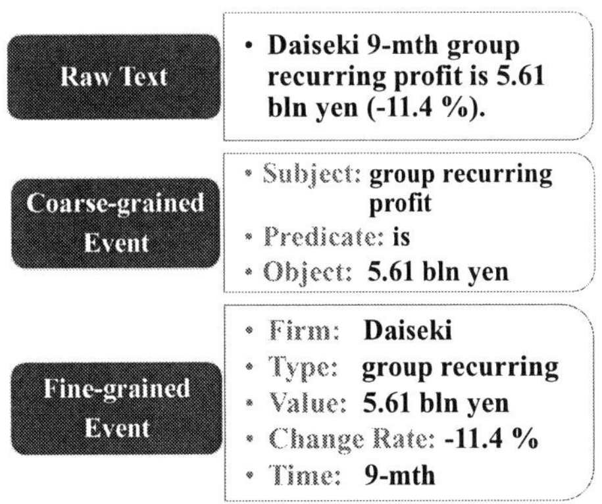

Figure 1: The same news of *Earnings Profit* event in different forms. The event structure consists of event roles (red words) which are the key point of the semantic information.

text (Ding et al., 2016; Zhang et al., 2018b). In the previous studies, the latter method has proven more powerful than the former one, which demonstrates that the event structure containing semantic information is helpful for stock movement prediction. Figure 1 shows a piece of news of *Earnings Profit* event in different forms: raw text, coarse-grained event (<S,P,O>) and fine-grained event (Yang et al., 2018; Liu et al., 2018). We observe that there are still some issues with the <S,P,O> method. Firstly, the <S,P,O> method only extracts subject, predicate and object, which misses some important event roles, such as the earnings *Time* and *Change Rate*, which are included in the fine-grained event. Besides, applying <S,P,O> structure for all event types loses the specific semantic structure in different types of finance events. In Figure 1, the fine-grained event employs *Type* instead of *Subject* used in the coarse-grained event and employs *Value* instead of *Object*, which can describe the event roles in a more detailed way. In this work, we propose to incorporate the fine-grained events in one-day-ahead stock movement prediction. The fine-grained

---

*This work is done when Deli Chen is a intern at Mizuho Securities.

Proceedings of the Second Workshop on Economics and Natural Language Processing, pages 31–40
Hong Kong, November 4. ©2019 Association for Computational Linguistics

event structure describes the specific framework and key points of various finance events. Applying fine-grained events is beneficial for learning a better text representation because the finance knowledge contained in event structure is helpful for understanding the semantic information.

Inspired by the automatic event data generation method (Chen et al., 2017; Zeng et al., 2018; Yang et al., 2018), we propose the TOPIX[1] Finance Event Dictionary (**TFED**) built by domain experts with professional finance knowledge and adopt it to extract fine-grained events automatically for most of finance news. Then we design two different neural models: Structured Stock Prediction Model (**SSPM**) and Multi-task Structured Stock Prediction Model (**MSSPM**). SSPM fuses the extracted fine-grained event and news text firstly, and then conduct interaction between text data and stock trade data to make prediction. SSPM outperforms all the baselines but it can hardly handle the news that can not be recognized by TFED, which we call uncovered news, so MSSPM is designed to learn event extraction using the fine-grained events as the distant supervised label. Besides, we propose to learn event extraction and stock prediction jointly in MSSPM because these two tasks are highly related. The improvement of event extraction result can boost news understanding and promote the stock prediction. And the output of stock prediction can give feedback to event extraction. So the joint learning can share valuable information between tasks. Result shows that MSSPM outperforms SSPM on the uncovered news and increases the method's generalizability. The contributions of this work are summarized as follows:

- We propose to incorporate the fine-grained events in stock movement prediction and this method outperforms all the baselines.

- We propose to learn event extraction and stock prediction jointly, which improves the method generalizability for uncovered news.

- We propose TFED and a pipeline method which can extract fine-grained events from finance news automatically.

- We propose the embedding method for minute-level stock trade data, and adopt time-series models to learn its representation.

---

[1]Tokyo Stock Price Index, commonly known as TOPIX, is an important stock market index for the Tokyo Stock Exchange (TSE) in Japan.

2 Related Work

2.1 Automatically Event Data Labeling

According to (Chen et al., 2015; Liu et al., 2018; Huang et al., 2018), the fine-grained event structure contains event types, event trigger words and event roles. Zhou et al. (2015) propose a framework to extract events from twitter automatically. Yang et al. (2018) employ a predefined dictionary to label events and then extract document-level events from Chinese finance news. However, they only conduct experiments on 4 event types. While we employ a widely-covered dictionary with 32 different event types. Chen et al. (2017) adopt world and linguistic knowledge to detect event roles and trigger words from text. Zeng et al. (2018) use the Freebase CVT structure to label data and extract event. Araki and Mitamura (2018) adopt distant supervision to extract event from open domain. There are some works using either manual rules (Arendarenko and Kakkonen, 2012) or machine learning methods (Jacobs et al., 2018) for finance event detection, while our event labeling method is stock specific with professional domain knowledge.

2.2 Stock Movement Prediction

Many works using related text for stock movement prediction take the raw text as model input directly. Xu and Cohen (2018) adopt a variational generation model to combine tweets and stock history data to make the prediction. Si et al. (2014) employ the sentiment analysis to help the decision. Li et al. (2015) adopt the tensor decompose method to get the interaction information of different inputs. Duan et al. (2018) use the summary of news body instead of news headline to predict the stock returns. Some other works try to employ structure information to predict the stock movement. Ding et al. (2014) extract <S,P,O> (subject, predicate and object) structure from news to predict the stock movement. Then they propose two improved method based on <S,P,O> structure by applying the weighted fusion of event roles (Ding et al., 2015) and introducing the entity relation knowledge (Ding et al., 2016). Besides, Zhang et al. (2018b) employ a RBM to process <S,P,O> to get the event representation.

3 Fine-grained Event Extraction

3.1 TOPIX Finance Event Dictionary

As shown in (Yang et al., 2018; Zeng et al., 2018) automatic fine-grained event extraction needs an event dictionary to define the event types. Each event type consists of event trigger words and event roles. News containing trigger words perhaps belongs to this event type. The event roles are the key points of semantic structure of this event type. However, there is no specific event dictionary for stock related finance events. So we hired three domain experts to summarize the high-frequency finance events which have a significant impact on stock trading and determine the event trigger words and event roles. With help of domain experts, we also annotated some auxiliary information for the following event extraction process: the POS label of the event roles, the dependency relation pattern of the event types and the necessary/unnecessary label of event roles. Not all event roles will appear in every instance of this event type. Take the *Earnings Profit* event in Figure 1 for example, the *Firm*, *Type* and *Value* will appear in every *Earnings Profit* instance. But the *Change Rate* and *Time* may not appear in some *Earnings Profit* instances. We regard the news containing all the necessary roles as an instance of related event.

TFED contains 32 types of finance events in 8 categories and covers all the main types of finance events that are highly related to stock movement, such as *Earnings Profit*, *M&A* and *Credit Ratings*. All the 32 event types of TFED are displayed in supplementary material A, as well as their trigger words and event roles.

3.2 Event Extraction Process

There are 4 steps in the event extraction process, in which we extract the fine-grained event structures from finance news.

1. Extract Auxiliary Information. In this step, we extract the auxiliary information of news: **POS Tagging** (lexical information) and **Dependency Relation** (syntactic information) by the popular Standford CoreNLP[2] (Manning et al., 2014).

2. Filter Event Candidates. We filter the news that may be an event instance by the TFED. News that contains any trigger word(s) in the dictionary will be regarded as a candidate of the related event.

For example, the news in the Figure 1 is a candidate for the *Earnings Profit* event because it contains the trigger word *profit*.

3. Locate Event Roles. We regard news containing all the necessary event roles as an event instance. For event candidates driven by trigger words, we adopt matching rules set by domain experts to check the dependency relation and POS information. Firstly, we match the dependency relation of the candidate news with predefined dependency relation pattern of this event type in TFED to locate the event roles and check if all the necessary event roles are recalled. Then we check if all the event roles' POS labels are consistent with predefined labels. Only if these two conditions are satisfied, this news will be regarded as an event instance and the event roles are determined.

4. BIO Post-process. The result of Step 3 is the label for event roles. Since we want to get the event label for each word in news, we use the BIO label standard to normalize the labeling result. After all these 4 steps, we access the fine-grained event of news. And the extraction result shows that our method covers 71% news in the 210k samples, which proves that the TFED and the pipeline method work well on our experiment data. And for uncovered news, adding more event types is of high cost and low efficiency, so we extract the $<$S,P,O$>$ structure as replacement following the approach in (Zhang et al., 2018b).

4 Proposed Method

4.1 Problem Formulation

Given N samples in the dataset, and the i-th sample (x^i, y^i, e^i, s^i) contains the news text x^i, the stock trade data y^i in the day before news happens, the event role label e^i generated in Section 3.2 and stock movement label s^i. $x^i = \left\{x_1^i, x_2^i, ..., x_L^i\right\}$ is a sequence of words with length of L. $e^i = \left\{e_1^i, e_2^i, ..., e_L^i\right\}$ is a sequence of labels indicating the event role of each word in x^i. $y^i = \left\{y_1^i, y_2^i, ..., y_M^i\right\}$ is a sequence of trade record vectors for each trade minute with length of M. $s^i \in \{0, 1\}$ is the stock movement label telling whether the stock trade price is up or down at prediction time. The stock movement prediction task can be defined as assigning movement label for the news input and trade data input.

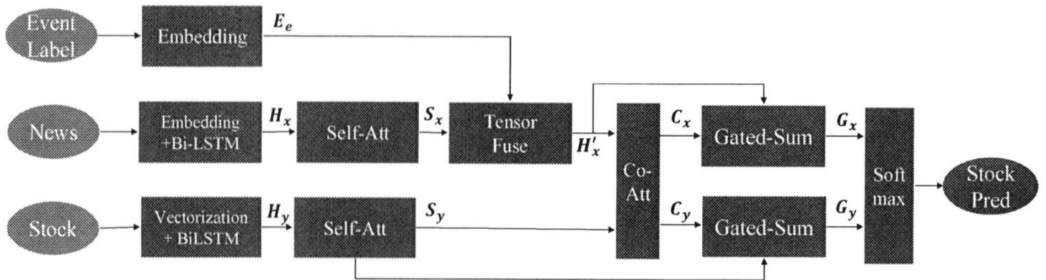

Figure 2: The overview of the proposed SSPM model.

4.2 Trade Data Embedding

Different from works of (Xu and Cohen, 2018; Zhang et al., 2018b) who use limited daily-level stock trade data (stock close price and daily trade volume, for example), we adopt the minute-level stock data to describe the stock movement in a more detailed way. For each minute when at least one trade happens, we collect the following items: (1) First/last/highest/lowest trade price of the minute; (2) Total trade volume/value of the minute; (3) Volume-weighted average trade price. The stock trade data is of time series data, so in order to apply the powerful time series neural models, we transfer the raw trade features into trade data embedding E_y. The following combination performs best on the develop set:

- Raw Number: first/last/highest/lowest trade price, total trade volume and volume-weighted average trade price

- Change Rate: change rates of all the raw number items compared to last minute

Now we get 12 feature numbers for each trade minute. We set the length of time step to 10 minutes. Then we get the trade data embedding $E_y \in \mathbb{R}^{T \times D_s}$. $T = \text{M}/10$ and $D_s = 120$. M is the length of the trade minutes. Finally, we adopt the min-max scale method for each stock's samples and pad the time steps less than 10 minutes with last trade minute's data.

4.3 Base Model: Structured Stock Prediction Model (SSPM)

Figure 2 shows the overview of SSPM. We first transfer various sources of input (x, y, e) into dense vectors. Then we get the representations of text and stock data through bi-directional Long Short Term Memory (BiLSTM) and self-attention. Then we fuse text and event structure to access the structure-aware text representation. Finally, we in-

teract text and stock data by co-attention to predict stock movement. There are 4 modules in SSPM: input embedding, single-modal information representation, bi-modal information interaction and prediction. Experiment results show that SSPM outperforms all the baselines.

4.3.1 Input Embedding

The purpose of this module is to transfer various sources of input (x, y, e) into dense vectors. For words in finance news x, we use both word-level pretrained embedding Glove (Pennington et al., 2014) and character-level pretrained embedding ELMo (Peters et al., 2018) for the purpose of representing words better from different levels. Then we concatenate them to get the final word representation $E_x \in \mathbb{R}^{L \times D_w}$. We use the method proposed in Section 4.2 to get the stock trade data embedding $E_y \in \mathbb{R}^{T \times D_s}$. Besides, we embed event role labels e into dense vectors $E_e \in \mathbb{R}^{L \times D_e}$ using a parameter matrix initialized with random values. D_w, D_s, D_e are the embedding dimensions of word, stock and event role, respectively. T is the length of stock time-steps.

4.3.2 Single-modal Information Representation

The purpose of this module is to get the representations for both news and stock trade data independently. After accessing the input embedding, we employ BiLSTM to encode the E_x and E_y :

$$H_x = \text{BiLSTM}_x(E_x)$$
$$H_y = \text{BiLSTM}_y(E_y)$$

Now we access the sentence representation $H_x \in \mathbb{R}^{L \times 2h}$ and daily stock trade representation $H_y \in \mathbb{R}^{T \times 2h}$. h is the hidden size of BiLSTM. In order to enhance the learning ability, we use the self-attention to allow the H_x and H_y to have a look at themselves and make adjustment. We apply the bi-linear attention method which have proven (Wang et al., 2018; Deng et al., 2018) more powerful in learning ability. Here are the formulas for H_x:

$$W_{SA}^x = \text{softmax}(\boldsymbol{H_x} \cdot W_1 \cdot \boldsymbol{H_x}^\top)$$
$$\boldsymbol{S_x} = W_{SA}^x \cdot \boldsymbol{H_x}$$

W_1 is a trainable weight matrix and $\boldsymbol{S_x} \in \mathbb{R}^{L \times 2h}$. In the same way we get the self-attention result of the stock data: $\boldsymbol{S_y} \in \mathbb{R}^{T \times 2h}$.

In the <S,P,O> method, event roles are extracted as separated phrases where some words are ignored and the word order information is missing. Instead, we fuse the text representation S_x with the event role embedding E_e to capture the structure information and remain the word order at the same time. E_e contains both word-level (event role) and sentence-level (BIO label) information, which is similar with S_x, so we select to fuse E_e with S_x instead of E_x. Here we adopt the fusion function used in (Wang et al., 2018; Mou et al., 2016) to fuse the event structure and text effectively:

$$\boldsymbol{H'_x} = \sigma(W_f[\boldsymbol{S_x}; \boldsymbol{E_e}; \boldsymbol{S_x} - \boldsymbol{E_e}; \boldsymbol{S_x} \circ \boldsymbol{E_e}] + b_f)$$

; means tensor connection. We ensure $D_e = 2h$ so that E_e has the same dimension with S_x. $\circ$ means element-wise multiplication and σ is the activation function. $\boldsymbol{H'_x} \in \mathbb{R}^{L \times 2h}$ is the structure-aware text representation.

4.3.3 Bi-modal Information Interaction

In this part we conduct the interaction between the two modal information: finance news of text mode and stock trade data of number mode. These two different modal information are highly relevant: the finance news represents the environment variable and the stock trade data represents history movement. The interaction between them can lead to a better understanding of stock movement. We use the co-attention to interact the bi-modal information: $\boldsymbol{H'_x} = \left\{h_x'^1, h_x'^2, \cdots, h_x'^L\right\}$ and $\boldsymbol{S_y} = \left\{s_y^1, s_y^2, \cdots, s_y^T\right\}$. The attention weight is computed by the following function:

$$f_{att}(i, j) = \text{Relu}(h_x'^{i\top} W_2 s_y^j)$$

W_2 is a trainable weight matrix. We use the softmax function to normalize the attention weight:

$$\alpha_{ij} = \frac{e^{f_{att}(i,j)}}{\sum_{k=1}^{T} e^{f_{att}(i,k)}}; \quad \beta_{ij} = \frac{e^{f_{att}(i,j)}}{\sum_{t=1}^{L} e^{f_{att}(t,j)}}$$

Finally we get the reconstructed representations:

$$c_x^i = \sum_{j=1}^{T} \alpha_{ij} \, s_y^j; \quad c_y^j = \sum_{i=1}^{L} \beta_{ij} \, h_x'^i$$

Now we access the reconstructed representations $\boldsymbol{C_x} = \left\{c_x^1, c_x^2, \cdots, c_x^L\right\}$ and $\boldsymbol{C_y} = \left\{c_y^1, c_y^2, \cdots, c_y^T\right\}$ based on the attention to another modal information. Then we use the gating mechanism to incorporate the original representation and the corresponding attention result:

$$\boldsymbol{G_x} = g(\boldsymbol{H'_x}, \boldsymbol{C_x}) \cdot \boldsymbol{C_x} + (1 - g(\boldsymbol{H'_x}, \boldsymbol{C_x})) \cdot \boldsymbol{H'_x}$$
$$\boldsymbol{G_y} = g(\boldsymbol{S_y}, \boldsymbol{C_y}) \cdot \boldsymbol{C_y} + (1 - g(\boldsymbol{S_y}, \boldsymbol{C_y})) \cdot \boldsymbol{S_y}$$

where the $g(,)$ is the gating function and we use the non-linear transformation with $sigmod$ activation function in experiment.

4.3.4 Prediction

In this module, we concatenate the $\boldsymbol{G_x}$ and $\boldsymbol{G_y}$ and predict the stock movement label $\widehat{p}$:

$$\widehat{p}(s|x, y, e) = \text{softmax}(W_p[\boldsymbol{G_x}; \boldsymbol{G_y}] + b_p)$$

4.4 Advanced Model: Multi-task Structured Stock Prediction Model (MSSPM)

SSPM can hardly process the uncovered news that can not be recognized by the TFED since the fine-grained event structure information is not provided. MSSPM is designed to handle this issue by employing the generated e in Section 3.2 as the distant supervised label to train an event extractor. Furthermore, we design a multi-task framework to jointly learn event extraction and stock prediction because these two tasks are highly related. The quality of event extraction result has a direct influence on the downstream stock prediction task. At the same time, the results of stock prediction can give valuable feedback to event extraction. The multi-task framework can share useful information and make effective interaction between tasks. The overview of MSSPM is shown in Figure 3. The upper half of the dotted line represents the event extraction part. We regard the event extraction task as a sequence labeling task and adopt the self-attended BiLSTM-CRF (conditional random fields) method to make labeling decisions. The lower half stands for the stock movement prediction part which works in a similar way as SSPM.

4.4.1 Event Extraction

After accessing the word embedding $\boldsymbol{E_x}$, we employ the BiLSTM to get the sentence representation $\boldsymbol{H_x}$. Then we employ self-attention to learn a better representation $\boldsymbol{S_x}$. Finally we predict the

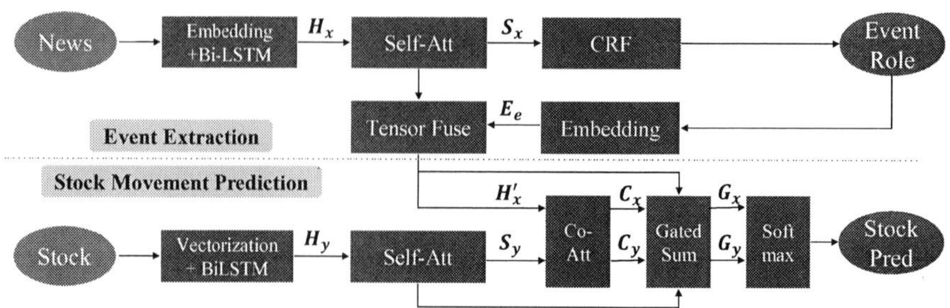

Figure 3: The overview of the proposed MSSPM model.

event label and employ CRF to optimize output:

$$\widehat{e} = \mathrm{softmax}(W_l\,\boldsymbol{S_x} + b_l)$$

$$\widehat{e'} = \mathrm{CRF}(\widehat{e})$$

$\widehat{e'}$ is the estimation of the event role. Then we adopt the method introduced in Section 4.3.1 to get the event role embedding $\boldsymbol{E_e}$ from $\widehat{e'}$ and adopt the tensor fusion function used in SSPM to get the structure-aware text representation $\boldsymbol{H'_x}$.

4.4.2 Stock Movement Prediction

The stock movement prediction process is similar with SSPM, and the main difference is the event input $\boldsymbol{E_e}$ is predicted from the event extractor in Section 4.4.1. The stock trade representation $\boldsymbol{S_y}$ is accessed in the same way with SSPM. Then we employ the co-attention to interact $\boldsymbol{H'_x}$ and $\boldsymbol{S_y}$, followed by the gated sum and $softmax$ function to predict the stock movement label $\widehat{s}$.

4.4.3 Multi-task Learning Object

The loss function of MSSPM consists of two parts, which are the negative logarithm loss of event extraction and that of stock prediction:

$$LS_e = -\sum_t e_t log\, p(e_t|x),\ t = [1,\cdots,L]$$

$$LS_s = -s \log p(s|x,y)$$

We select the weighted sum of these two losses as the final loss of MSSPM:

$$LS = \lambda LS_e/L + (1 - \lambda)LS_s$$

The λ is a hyper-parameter to balance two losses. LS_e is divided by the number of words to ensure it is comparable with LS_s. The experiment result shows that model performs best on develop set when $\lambda = 0.43$.

5 Experiment

The experiment data is from the professional finance news providers Reuters[3]. We collect finance news related to TOPIX top 1000 stocks[4] from 2011 to 2017. The raw data contains both news headline and body, and we use headline only since the headline contains the most valuable information and has less noise than news body. We collect stock trade data for news happens in/out of trade time (9:00 AM - 15:00 PM in trade day) differently. For those news happens in trade time, we collect the trade data from 9:00 AM to the last minute before news happens. And for those news happens out of trade time, we collect the trade data of last trade day. We want to ensure no trade data after news happens are included in the input in which situation the market reactions are leaked to the model. We get about 210k data samples finally. Following (Ding et al., 2015; Xu and Cohen, 2018), the stock movement is divided into two categories: stock up/down. The stock up and down rates are 45% and 55% in our dataset, respectively. We adopt TOPIX Sector Index to correct the stock movement in order to eliminate the influence of macro news and the details are introduced in supplementary materials C. In experiment, we reserve 10k samples for developing and 10k samples for testing. The samples in train set are previous to samples in valid set and test set to avoid the possible information leakage. All the rest 190k samples are applied for training SSPM while only the dictionary covered part (about 70%) in the 190k samples are applied for training MSSPM to acquire a high-quality event extractor. We tune the hyper-parameters on the development set and

---

[3]Source Reuters News cThomson Reuters cREFINITIV, https://www.thomsonreuters.com/en.html

[4]Each news in Reuters has a manual field indicating its related stock(s) and we use it to filter the stock related news.

test model on the test set. The evaluation metrics are accuracy and Matthews Correlation Coefficient (MCC). MCC is often used in stock forecast (Xu and Cohen, 2018; Ding et al., 2016) because it can overcome the data imbalance issue. More experiment details are listed in the supplementary material D.

6 Results and Analysis

We analyze the results of experiments in this section. Firstly, we compare the proposed methods with the baselines in Section 6.1. Then we analyze the effect of event structure input in SSPM in Section 6.2 and analyze the MSSPM method in Section 6.3. Lastly, we conduct the ablation study in Section 6.4. We also conduct error analysis over different times' news, which is shown in the supplementary material B.

6.1 Comparison With Baselines

The following baselines are used in this work.

- **Bagging Decision Tree:** This method adopt bagging ensemble algorithm to combine 20 Decision Tree classifiers to make the prediction. It outperforms all the other traditional machine learning methods we tried.

- **Sentiment Analysis:** This method (Si et al., 2014) conducts sentiment analysis on news headlines to predict stock movement.

- **Target Specific Representation:** This method (Duan et al., 2018) employs the news headline as the target to summarize the news body in order to utilize the abundant information of news body.

- **Triple Structure:** This method (Ding et al., 2014) adopts the $<$S,P,O$>$ triple to represent the event structure.

- **Weighted Triple Structure:** This method (Ding et al., 2015) adds trainable weight matrices in $<$S,P,O$>$ to enhance fitting ability.

- **Triple Structure with RBM:** This method (Zhang et al., 2018b) uses Restricted Boltzmann Machine to handle the $<$S,P,O$>$ and then adopts multi-instance learning to model the latent consistencies of different data sources. Because tweet data are contained in news data[5] in our dataset, our implementa-

---

[5]Some related tweets about stocks are also provided by Reuters mixed with news.

Method	Event	Acc(%)	MCC
Bagging Decision Tree	No	54.9	0.096
Sentiment Analysis (Si et al., 2014)	No	62.8	0.253
Target Specific Rep. (Duan et al., 2018)	No	63.7	0.275
Triple Structure (Ding et al., 2014)	Coarse-grained	63.2	0.270
Weighted Triple Structure (Ding et al., 2015)	Coarse-grained	63.5	0.269
Triple Structure with RBM (Zhang et al., 2018b)	Coarse-grained	64.0	0.278
MSSPM(proposed)	Fine-grained	65.7	0.315
SSPM(proposed)	Fine-grained	66.4	0.330
Ensemble	Fine-grained	**67.2**	**0.348**

Table 1: Results on test set compared with baselines; the results in this table and following tables have proven significant with $p < 0.05$ by student t-test.

tion uses news and stock data instead of news, tweet and stock data.

Table 1 is divided into three parts. The three baselines in the top part employ the text directly as model input. These methods totally ignore the structure information of text. The three baselines in the middle part take structure information into account. These methods consider $<$S,P,O$>$ event roles in all event types though, they miss some important event roles and describe the event roles in a very rough way. Moreover, the word order information is missing under such settings. Both SSPM and MSSPM outperform all the baselines. These proposed method incorporate the fine-grained event structure in stock movement prediction. It can extract specific fine-grained event structures for different types of finance events. At the same time, this method remains the original word order through the tensor fusion. Another advantage of our method is that it applies the stock data embedding method for the minute-level stock trade data and conducts interaction between stock data and news data. SSPM performs a little better than MSSPM because SSPM adopts more data for training and the learning of event extraction in MSSPM is not perfect. The Ensemble method follows a simple rule to combine the SSPM and MSSPM: The TFED covered news is processed by SSPM and the uncovered news is processed by MSSPM. It achieves the best result among all the baselines and proposed methods.

6.2 Effect of Event Structure

In this section, we analyze the effect of event structure. Although there have been some comparisons of different event structures in Section 6.1,

Input Form	Acc(%)	MCC
No Text	58.1	0.161
No Event (Raw Text)	62.2	0.246
Coarse-grained Event	64.6	0.291
Fine-grained Event	**66.4**	**0.330**

Table 2: Different Text Input Forms in SSPM.

Data	Covered		Uncovered	
Metric	Acc(%)	MCC	Acc(%)	MCC
SSPM	67.6	0.351	63.4	0.267
MSSPM	65.9	0.318	**65.2**	**0.305**

Table 3: Result on different sets of test data. The covered set means samples recognized by the TFED and the uncovered set means the samples out of the dictionary. These two sets account for around 30% and 70% of the test set, respectively.

Task	Event Extraction	Stock Prediction	
Metric	Micro-F1(%)	Acc(%)	MCC
Pipeline	79.2	64.8	0.297
Multi-Task	**84.3**	**65.7**	**0.315**

Table 4: Comparison of pipeline method and multi-task learning method (MSSPM). The pipeline method trains the event extractor first and then predicts the stock. We report the micro-F1 score for the event extraction task.

the models are different. In this section, we conduct an experiment based on the SSPM model and change different text input forms to check the impact of the event structure. We design 4 different text input forms for SSPM: (1) No Text method takes no text information as input and relies entirely on trade data to predict stock movement; (2) No Event takes the raw news text as model input and removes the event input from SSPM; (3) Coarse-grained Event employs the coarse-grained event structure $<$S, P, O$>$ as event input of SSPM; (4) Fine-grained Event is the proposed method to utilize the category-specific fine-grained event as model input. The results are shown in Table 2. We can find that all the there methods adding text input outperform the No Text method, which proves the effect of finance news. Both the Coarse-grained and Fine-grained Event methods bring improvement to the prediction result, which shows that the event structure is very useful. Moreover, the Fine-grained Event method brings larger improvement than the Coarse-grained Event method, which demonstrates that utilizing fine-grained events is more helpful to help model understanding the semantic information of news text.

6.3 Analysis of MSSPM

Although SSPM performs well in stock prediction, there are two important issues with it. Firstly, 29% news in our dataset can not be recognized by TFED, and the Table 3 shows that the result of uncovered data is obvious lower than the covered data. Secondly, TFED is domain specific, so the generalizability of SSPM may be restricted. MSSPM is designed to handle these two issues.

As shown in Table 3, although the performance of MSSPM is lower than SSPM on the covered test set, its performance is higher than SSPM on the uncovered test set. The performance decrease of MSSPM after transferring from covered set to uncovered set is much smaller than SSPM's, which proves MSSPM has higher transferability. The uncovered news can be regarded as events of new types, and MSSPM performs better on it by learn-

ing event extraction, which improves the generalizability of the structured stock prediction method. As shown in Table 4, the performance of multi-task learning is clearly better than the pipeline method, which confirms our assumption that these two tasks are highly related and the joint learning improves both of their results.

6.4 Ablation Study

In this section, we report and analyze the results of ablation study. We remove different components of both SSPM and MSSPM to check their effect. As shown in Table 5 and Table 6, we found that the model performance drops in all the ablation experiments as expected. The fusion function, attention mechanism (both self-attention and co-attention) and the gating mechanism are all helpful for both SSPM and MSSPM. We can observe an obvious decrease after removing fusion function (adopt adding method instead) both in SSPM ($\downarrow$ 1.5 of Acc) and MSSPM ($\downarrow$ 1.1 of Acc), which demonstrates that the fusion function combines the event structure and the news text effectively. Besides, the co-attention between news and stock trade data also plays an important role in both models.

7 Conclusion

In this work, we propose to incorporate the fine-grained events in stock movement prediction task. We propose the TOPIX Finance Event Dictionary with domain experts' knowledge and extract fine-grained events automatically. We propose SSPM

Metric	Acc(%)	MCC
SSPM	**66.4**	**0.330**
w/o Fusion Function	64.9($\downarrow$ 1.5)	0.298($\downarrow$ 0.032)
w/o Self-Attention	66.0($\downarrow$ 0.4)	0.319($\downarrow$ 0.011)
w/o Co-Attention	65.1($\downarrow$ 1.3)	0.303($\downarrow$ 0.027)
w/o Gated Sum	65.6($\downarrow$ 0.8)	0.314($\downarrow$ 0.016)

Table 5: Ablation Study of SSPM.

Metric	Acc(%)	MCC
MSSPM	**65.7**	**0.315**
w/o Fusion Function	64.6($\downarrow$ 1.1)	0.292($\downarrow$ 0.023)
w/o Self-Attention	65.5($\downarrow$ 0.2)	0.310($\downarrow$ 0.005)
w/o Co-Attention	64.9($\downarrow$ 0.8)	0.298($\downarrow$ 0.017)
w/o Gated Sum	65.2($\downarrow$ 0.5)	0.304($\downarrow$ 0.011)
w/o CRF	64.2($\downarrow$ 1.5)	0.285($\downarrow$ 0.030)

Table 6: Ablation Study of MSSPM.

to incorporate fine-grained events in stock movement prediction which outperforms all the baselines. Besides, to handle the uncovered news, we use the event data as the distant supervised label to train a multi-task framework MSSPM. The results show that MSSPM performs better on uncovered news and improves the generalizability of the structured stock prediction method.

8 Acknowledgement

This work is supported by a Research Grant from Mizuho Securities Co., Ltd. Three experienced stock traders from Mizuho Securities provide the professional support for the TFED dictionary. Mizuho Securities also provide experiment data.

References

Hana Alostad and Hasan Davulcu. 2017. Directional prediction of stock prices using breaking news on twitter. *Web Intelligence*, 15(1):1–17.

Jun Araki and Teruko Mitamura. 2018. Open-domain event detection using distant supervision. In *Proceedings of the 27th International Conference on Computational Linguistics, COLING 2018, Santa Fe, New Mexico, USA, August 20-26, 2018*, pages 878–891.

Ernest Arendarenko and Tuomo Kakkonen. 2012. Ontology-based information and event extraction for business intelligence. In *Artificial Intelligence: Methodology, Systems, and Applications - 15th International Conference, AIMSA 2012, Varna, Bulgaria, September 12-15, 2012. Proceedings*, pages 89–102.

Yubo Chen, Shulin Liu, Xiang Zhang, Kang Liu, and Jun Zhao. 2017. Automatically labeled data generation for large scale event extraction. In *Proceedings of the 55th Annual Meeting of the Association for Computational Linguistics, ACL 2017, Vancouver, Canada, July 30 - August 4, Volume 1: Long Papers*, pages 409–419.

Yubo Chen, Liheng Xu, Kang Liu, Daojian Zeng, and Jun Zhao. 2015. Event extraction via dynamic multi-pooling convolutional neural networks. In *Proceedings of the 53rd Annual Meeting of the Association for Computational Linguistics and the 7th International Joint Conference on Natural Language Processing of the Asian Federation of Natural Language Processing, ACL 2015, July 26-31, 2015, Beijing, China, Volume 1: Long Papers*, pages 167–176.

Yang Deng, Yuexiang Xie, Yaliang Li, Min Yang, Nan Du, Wei Fan, Kai Lei, and Ying Shen. 2018. Multi-task learning with multi-view attention for answer selection and knowledge base question answering. *CoRR*, abs/1812.02354.

Xiao Ding, Yue Zhang, Ting Liu, and Junwen Duan. 2014. Using structured events to predict stock price movement: An empirical investigation. In *Proceedings of the 2014 Conference on Empirical Methods in Natural Language Processing, EMNLP 2014, October 25-29, 2014, Doha, Qatar, A meeting of SIGDAT, a Special Interest Group of the ACL*, pages 1415–1425.

Xiao Ding, Yue Zhang, Ting Liu, and Junwen Duan. 2015. Deep learning for event-driven stock prediction. In *Proceedings of the Twenty-Fourth International Joint Conference on Artificial Intelligence, IJCAI 2015, Buenos Aires, Argentina, July 25-31, 2015*, pages 2327–2333.

Xiao Ding, Yue Zhang, Ting Liu, and Junwen Duan. 2016. Knowledge-driven event embedding for stock prediction. In *COLING 2016, 26th International Conference on Computational Linguistics, Proceedings of the Conference: Technical Papers, December 11-16, 2016, Osaka, Japan*, pages 2133–2142.

Junwen Duan, Yue Zhang, Xiao Ding, Ching-Yun Chang, and Ting Liu. 2018. Learning target-specific representations of financial news documents for cumulative abnormal return prediction. In *Proceedings of the 27th International Conference on Computational Linguistics, COLING 2018, Santa Fe, New Mexico, USA, August 20-26, 2018*, pages 2823–2833.

Ziniu Hu, Weiqing Liu, Jiang Bian, Xuanzhe Liu, and Tie-Yan Liu. 2018. Listening to chaotic whispers: A deep learning framework for news-oriented stock trend prediction. In *Proceedings of the Eleventh ACM International Conference on Web Search and Data Mining, WSDM 2018, Marina Del Rey, CA, USA, February 5-9, 2018*, pages 261–269.

Lifu Huang, Heng Ji, Kyunghyun Cho, Ido Dagan, Sebastian Riedel, and Clare R. Voss. 2018. Zero-shot transfer learning for event extraction. In *Proceedings of the 56th Annual Meeting of the Associa-

tion for Computational Linguistics, ACL 2018, Melbourne, Australia, July 15-20, 2018, Volume 1: Long Papers, pages 2160–2170.

Gilles Jacobs, Els Lefever, and Véronique Hoste. 2018. Economic event detection in company-specific news text. In *The 56th Annual Meeting of the Association for Computational Linguistics*, pages 1–10. Association for Computational Linguistics.

Qing Li, LiLing Jiang, Ping Li, and Hsinchun Chen. 2015. Tensor-based learning for predicting stock movements. In *Proceedings of the Twenty-Ninth AAAI Conference on Artificial Intelligence, January 25-30, 2015, Austin, Texas, USA.*, pages 1784–1790.

Xiao Liu, Zhunchen Luo, and Heyan Huang. 2018. Jointly multiple events extraction via attention-based graph information aggregation. In *Proceedings of the 2018 Conference on Empirical Methods in Natural Language Processing, Brussels, Belgium, October 31 - November 4, 2018*, pages 1247–1256.

Christopher D. Manning, Mihai Surdeanu, John Bauer, Jenny Finkel, Steven J. Bethard, and David McClosky. 2014. The Stanford CoreNLP natural language processing toolkit. In *Association for Computational Linguistics (ACL) System Demonstrations*, pages 55–60.

Lili Mou, Rui Men, Ge Li, Yan Xu, Lu Zhang, Rui Yan, and Zhi Jin. 2016. Natural language inference by tree-based convolution and heuristic matching. In *Proceedings of the 54th Annual Meeting of the Association for Computational Linguistics, ACL 2016, August 7-12, 2016, Berlin, Germany, Volume 2: Short Papers*.

Jeffrey Pennington, Richard Socher, and Christopher D. Manning. 2014. Glove: Global vectors for word representation. In *Empirical Methods in Natural Language Processing (EMNLP)*, pages 1532–1543.

Matthew E. Peters, Mark Neumann, Mohit Iyyer, Matt Gardner, Christopher Clark, Kenton Lee, and Luke Zettlemoyer. 2018. Deep contextualized word representations. In *Proceedings of the 2018 Conference of the North American Chapter of the Association for Computational Linguistics: Human Language Technologies, NAACL-HLT 2018, New Orleans, Louisiana, USA, June 1-6, 2018, Volume 1 (Long Papers)*, pages 2227–2237.

Jianfeng Si, Arjun Mukherjee, Bing Liu, Sinno Jialin Pan, Qing Li, and Huayi Li. 2014. Exploiting social relations and sentiment for stock prediction. In *Proceedings of the 2014 Conference on Empirical Methods in Natural Language Processing, EMNLP 2014, October 25-29, 2014, Doha, Qatar, A meeting of SIGDAT, a Special Interest Group of the ACL*, pages 1139–1145.

Wei Wang, Chen Wu, and Ming Yan. 2018. Multi-granularity hierarchical attention fusion networks for reading comprehension and question answering. In *Proceedings of the 56th Annual Meeting of the Association for Computational Linguistics, ACL 2018, Melbourne, Australia, July 15-20, 2018, Volume 1: Long Papers*, pages 1705–1714.

Yumo Xu and Shay B. Cohen. 2018. Stock movement prediction from tweets and historical prices. In *Proceedings of the 56th Annual Meeting of the Association for Computational Linguistics, ACL 2018, Melbourne, Australia, July 15-20, 2018, Volume 1: Long Papers*, pages 1970–1979.

Hang Yang, Yubo Chen, Kang Liu, Yang Xiao, and Jun Zhao. 2018. DCFEE: A document-level chinese financial event extraction system based on automatically labeled training data. In *Proceedings of ACL 2018, Melbourne, Australia, July 15-20, 2018, System Demonstrations*, pages 50–55.

Ying Zeng, Yansong Feng, Rong Ma, Zheng Wang, Rui Yan, Chongde Shi, and Dongyan Zhao. 2018. Scale up event extraction learning via automatic training data generation. In *Proceedings of the Thirty-Second AAAI Conference on Artificial Intelligence, (AAAI-18), the 30th innovative Applications of Artificial Intelligence (IAAI-18), and the 8th AAAI Symposium on Educational Advances in Artificial Intelligence (EAAI-18), New Orleans, Louisiana, USA, February 2-7, 2018*, pages 6045–6052.

Lingling Zhang, Saiji Fu, and Bochen Li. 2018a. Research on stock price forecast based on news sentiment analysis - A case study of alibaba. In *Computational Science - ICCS 2018 - 18th International Conference, Wuxi, China, June 11-13, 2018, Proceedings, Part II*, pages 429–442.

Xi Zhang, Siyu Qu, Jieyun Huang, Binxing Fang, and Philip S. Yu. 2018b. Stock market prediction via multi-source multiple instance learning. *IEEE Access*, 6:50720–50728.

Yunsong Zhong, Qinpei Zhao, and Weixiong Rao. 2017. Predicting stock market indexes with world news. In *4th International Conference on Systems and Informatics, ICSAI 2017, Hangzhou, China, November 11-13, 2017*, pages 1535–1540.

Deyu Zhou, Liangyu Chen, and Yulan He. 2015. An unsupervised framework of exploring events on twitter: Filtering, extraction and categorization. In *Proceedings of the Twenty-Ninth AAAI Conference on Artificial Intelligence, January 25-30, 2015, Austin, Texas, USA.*, pages 2468–2475.

Group, Extract and Aggregate: Summarizing a Large Amount of Finance News for Forex Movement Prediction

Deli Chen[1]*, Shuming Ma[1], Keiko Harimoto[2], Ruihan Bao[2], Qi Su[1], Xu Sun[1]

[1]MOE Key Lab of Computational Linguistics, School of EECS, Peking University
[2]Mizuho Securities Co., Ltd.
{chendeli,shumingma,sukia,xusun}@pku.edu.cn,
{keiko.harimoto,ruihan.bao}@mizuho-sc.com

Abstract

Incorporating related text information has proven successful in stock market prediction. However, it is a huge challenge to utilize texts in the enormous forex (foreign currency exchange) market because the associated texts are too redundant. In this work, we propose a BERT-based Hierarchical Aggregation Model to summarize a large amount of finance news to predict forex movement. We firstly group news from different aspects: time, topic and category. Then we extract the most crucial news in each group by the SOTA extractive summarization method. Finally, we conduct interaction between the news and the trade data with attention to predict the forex movement. The experimental results show that the category based method performs best among three grouping methods and outperforms all the baselines. Besides, we study the influence of essential news attributes (category and region) by statistical analysis and summarize the influence patterns for different currency pairs.

1 Introduction

Deep learning and Natural Language Processing technologies have been widely applied in market prediction tasks (Strauß et al., 2018; Alostad and Davulcu, 2017; Li et al., 2015; Ni et al., 2019), and the market related finance news has proven very useful for the prediction (Ding et al., 2016; Xu and Cohen, 2018). However, the studies of prediction in forex market, which is the largest market in the world with the highest daily trading volume, is much less than that in the stock market. Figure 1 shows the average numbers per hour of forex related news. There is a large amount of finance news related to forex trading with different influence, so it is a huge challenge to extract the useful semantic information from news. Most of previous works (Bakhach et al., 2016; Shen and Liang,

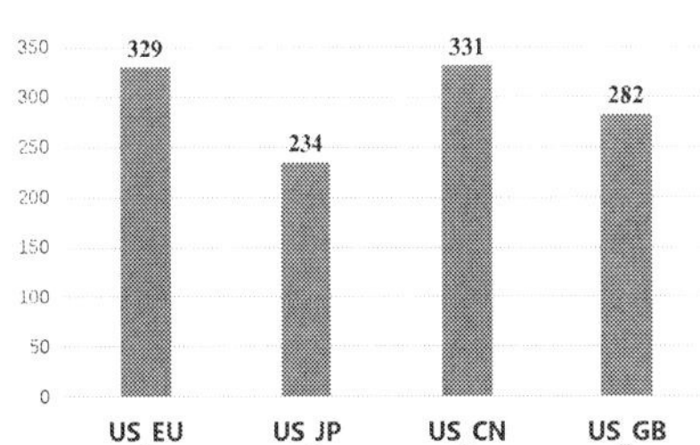

Figure 1: Average numbers per hour of forex related news from Reuters in 2013-2017. US_EU represents news related to US, Europe or both of them.

2016; Pradeepkumar and Ravi, 2016; Contreras et al., 2018; Weeraddana et al., 2018) on forex prediction ignore related text totally and focus on the forex trade data only, which loses the important semantic information. Yet existing works (Seifollahi and Shajari, 2019; Nassirtoussi et al., 2015) applying finance news in forex prediction mainly rely on manual rules to build feature vectors, which can hardly access the semantic information effectively.

To make better use of finance news, we propose a novel neural model: Bert-based Hierarchical Aggregation Model (**BHAM**) to summarize a large amount of finance news for forex movement prediction. We suppose that the finance news is redundant and only a small amount of news plays a crucial role in forex trading. So the key point is how to extract the most important news. In BHAM, we design a hierarchical structure to extract essential news at the group level first and then aggregate the semantic information across all groups. We expect the news is more related intra-group and less related inter-groups to make the extraction more effective. We design three grouping methods from different aspects: time, topic or category. At the group level, we concatenate news headlines in the same group and regard news extraction in each group as an extractive summarization task. We modify the SOTA extractive summarization model proposed in (Liu, 2019) to select the most important news. The connection process

---

*This work is done when Deli Chen is a intern at Mizuho Securities.

Proceedings of the Second Workshop on Economics and Natural Language Processing, pages 41–50
Hong Kong, November 4. ©2019 Association for Computational Linguistics

can let the selected news both content aware and context aware. Followingly, we conduct multimodal interaction between news data and trade data through attention mechanism to predict the forex prediction. The trade data represents the history movement of the forex, and the news data represents the environment variable. These two types of information are highly related.

We conduct experiments on four major currency pairs (USD-EUR, USD-JPY, USD-RMB, USD-GBP), and the experimental results show that the category-based BHAM performs best among all the baselines and proposed methods in all currency pairs. Based on this method, we analyze the influence of input time and prediction time on forex trading. We also analyze the influence of news category and news region and find various influence patterns for different currency pairs, which may be enlightening to the forex investors. The main contributions of this works are summarized as follows:

- We design a novel neural model to incorporate finance news in forex movement prediction. To the best of our knowledge, this is the first work to use the neural model to summarize a large amount of news for forex movement prediction.

- We propose three news grouping methods from different aspects: time, topic and category. Experiments show that the category based method performs best and outperforms all the baselines.

- Based on our experiments, we study the effect of time parameters on forex trading. We also analyze and summarize different influence patterns of finance news (both category and region) on different currency pairs.

2 Related Work

BERT (Devlin et al., 2018) is a potent pretrained contextualized sentence representation and has proven obvious improvement for many NLP tasks (Sun et al., 2019; Xu et al., 2019). Liu (2019) proposes a modified BERT for extractive summarization and achieve the state-of-the-art result in extractive document summarization task.

There have been many studies applying the related text in market prediction tasks. Moreover, the text assisted stock movement prediction has attracted many researchers' interest. Most of these works predict stock movement based on single news: Si et al. (2014) utilize the sentiment analysis to help the prediction. Duan et al. (2018) adopt the summarization of news body instead of headline to predict. Ding et al. (2016) propose the knowledge-driven event embedding method to make the forecast. Yet some others choose multi-news: Hu et al. (2018) propose a hybrid attention network to combine news in different days. However, the number of combined news is still limited and much smaller than that of forex news.

Compared to stock prediction, works about forex prediction is much scarce, and most of these works (Carapuço et al., 2018; Bakhach et al., 2016; Yong et al., 2018; Roledene et al., 2016; Contreras et al., 2018; Weeraddana et al., 2018) do not consider the text information. Shen and Liang (2016) employ stacked autoencoder to get the trade data representation and adopt support vector regression to predict. de Almeida et al. (2018) combine SVM with genetic algorithms to optimize investments in Forex markets based on history price. Tsai et al. (2018) choose the convolutional neural network to process the trading data. Besides, only limited works utilize the forex related text in the prediction process. Nassirtoussi et al. (2015) adopt the WordNet (Miller, 1995) and SentiWordNet (Baccianella et al., 2010) to extract the text semantic and sentiment information and build the text feature vector to forecast forex movement. Following this work, Seifollahi and Shajari (2019) add word sense disambiguation in the sentiment analysis of news headlines. Vijayan and Potey (2016) apply the J48 algorithm in analyzing text. This kind of method pays more attention to access a fixed feature vector from news and can only represent news on a shallow level. In this work, we propose a selection and aggregation neural framework to process the larger amount of finance news and employ the powerful pre-trained BERT as text encoder, which can learn the deep semantic information effectively.

3 Approach

3.1 Problem Formulation

Each sample in the dataset (x, y, f) contains the set of news text x, the forex trade data y, and the forex movement label f. x and y happen in the same input time window. To be more specific, x is a list of news groups $x = \{C^1, C^2, \cdots, C^L\}$. L is the number of groups. The methods for

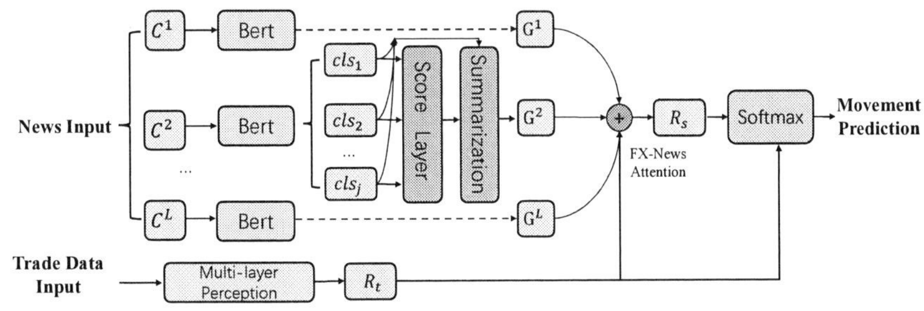

Figure 2: The overview of the proposed model.

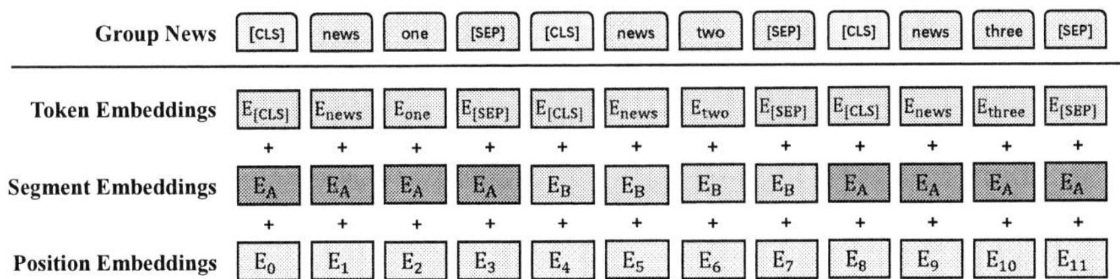

Figure 3: The BERT input in each news group.

dividing groups are introduced in Section 3.5. Each news group is a sequence of finance news $[news_1, news_2, \cdots, news_K]$ in chronological order. y is the trade data embedding accessed by the method introduced in Section 3.6. And $f \in \{1, 0\}$ is the forex movement label telling whether the forex trade price is up or down after a certain time (we call it prediction delay). The forex movement prediction task can be defined as assigning movement label for the news input and trade data input.

3.2 Model Overview

The overview of the Bert-based Hierarchical Aggregation Model (**BHAM**) is displayed in Figure 2. The model can be generally divided into two steps: (1)Intra-group extraction and (2)Inter-groups aggregation. In the Intra-group extraction step, news in the same group is connected as a continuous paragraph, and we conduct extractive summarization on this paragraph to select the most important news. Specifically, we employ BERT as the encoder to get the contextualized paragraph representation and compute the importance score for each news. Then we select and aggregate the top-k (k is a hyper-parameters) news to get the final group representation. In the Inter-groups aggregation step, we first access the trade data representation by a 3-layer perceptron and then employ the trade data representation as a query to calculate the attention scores of all the news group and obtain the final news representation. Finally, we fuse the final news representation and the trade

data representation to predict the forex movement.

3.3 Intra-group Extraction

There will be lots of news in the same group, and we suppose that only a small amount of news has the greatest influence on the forex movement. The purpose of this step is to select the essential news from all news in group, which is redundant and full of noise. Inspired by the BERT-based extractive summarization model proposed in (Liu, 2019), we modify this method to select the most crucial news in each group. All the news in the same group is related to the subject of this group, and the connection of them in chronological order can be regarded as the continuous description of the group subject. The connection can make the news representations realize the context information of this group by passing information among different news. We suppose the context information can help select better news in group.

The form of group news input for BERT encoder is illustrated in Figure 3. We insert a [CLS] token before each news and a [SEP] token after each news. For the segment embedding, we use the loop of $[E_A, E_B]$ to extend the raw segment embedding of BERT to multi-sentences. After the BERT encoding, all the [CLS] tokens *cls* are regarded as the semantic representations of the corresponding news. The importance score for each news is calculated base on these [CLS] tokens:

$$score^i = \text{sigmoid}(W_0 * cls^i + b_0) \quad (1)$$

$$t^i = \text{TOP}_\text{k}(score^i) \quad (2)$$

$$s^i = \text{softmax}(t^i) \quad (3)$$

Where $i \in \{1, 2, \cdots, L\}$, L is the number of groups. cls^i is the list of [CLS] tokens in the i-th group. W_0 and b_0 are the trainable parameters. $score^i$ is a list of values indicating the important scores of news. TOP_k is an operation to select the top-k pieces of news with the highest scores. Then the group representation is calculated by the weighted sum of the top-k [CLS] tokens:

$$G^i = \sum_{j=1}^{k} cls^i_j * s^i_j \quad (4)$$

The G^i is the final representation of the i-th news group which contains the semantic information from the most important news in this group.

3.4 Inter-groups Aggregation

The purpose of this step is to aggregate semantic information at the inter-groups level. The forex trade data and the finance news are highly relevant: the trade data represents the history movement of forex, and the finance news represents the environmental variable. So the combination of them can help us model the forex movement better. In a certain input time, news groups have different impacts on forex movement. So we employ the trade data as a query to calculate the attention weights of news groups. Then the weighted sum of news groups and the trade data representation are finally fused to predict the forex movement. For forex trade data y, we apply a 3-layer perceptron to access the trade data representation R_t, and each layer is a non-linear transform with Relu activation function. Then we calculate the attention weight between R_t and G^i :

$$g(i) = \text{Relu}(R_t * W_a * G^{i\top}) \quad (5)$$

$$att_i = \frac{e^{g(i)}}{\sum_{i=1}^{L} e^{g(i)}} \quad (6)$$

Where $att(i)$ is the i-th news group's attention weight to trade data. Then we sum the news groups representations up to get the final news semantic representation R_s:

$$R_s = \sum_{i=1}^{L} G^i * att_i \quad (7)$$

To fuse the news semantic and trade data representations effectively, we choose the fusion function used in (Wang et al., 2018; Mou et al., 2016) to fuse R_s and R_t and predict the movement:

$$R = [R_t; R_s; R_t - R_s; R_t \circ R_s] \quad (8)$$

$$\widehat{p}(f|x, y) = \text{softmax}(W_p * R + b_p) \quad (9)$$

$\circ$ means element-wise multiplication.

3.5 Methods of Grouping News

In this part, we introduce the three news grouping methods. The ideal division enables news groups to be high cohesion and low coupling, which means the semantic information of finance news should be highly related intra-group and less related inter-groups. We suppose that extracting news by groups can reduce the extraction difficulty compared to extracting from all news directly because news in the same group is close to each other and has less noise. Moreover, this method can help us analyze the contributions of different groups.

3.5.1 Grouping by Time

In this method, finance news is divided into groups according to the time when news happens. We set the time unit to 5 minutes and news released in the same time unit will be divided into the same group. This method supposes that news happened closely is highly correlated.

3.5.2 Grouping by Topic

In this method, finance news is divided into groups by news topic. The news topics are generated by unsupervised news clustering. In this work, we choose the affinity propagation algorithm (Frey and Dueck, 2007) to generate news clusters without setting the number of clusters subjectively. Moreover, we choose the tf-idf of 2-gram features from news headlines. This method supposes that finance news focuses on several finance event topics at a particular time. News in the same topic describes this topic from different aspects and has a high correlation.

3.5.3 Grouping by Category

In this method, news is divided into groups by category. The news categories[1] are {Business Sectors, Business General, Business Assets, Business Commodities, Business Organizations, Politics&International Affairs,

---

[1] Use the Reuters professional financial news category(https://liaison.reuters.com/tools/topic-codes) and merge some similar categories.

Arts&Culture&Entertainment&Sports, Science &Technology, Other}. This method supposes that news in the same category is close to each other.

3.6 Trade Data Embedding

The raw record of forex data includes the open/ close/high/low trade prices for each minute. In order to extract all the possible features, we build the trade data embedding y containing multi aspects:

- **Raw Number**: open/close/high/low trade price for each trade minute.

- **Change Rate**: change rate of open/close/ high/low price compared to last trade minute.

- **Trade Statistics**: mean value, max value, min value, median, variance of all the trade prices in input minutes.

The min-max scale is applied for each currency pair's samples to scale the raw numbers in y to $[0, 1]$ according to the maximum and minimum value of each feature.

3.7 Training Objective

The loss function of the proposed model includes two parts: the negative log-likelihood training loss and the L_2 regularization item:

$$Loss = -f * log\, p(f|x, y, \theta) + \frac{\lambda}{2} \|\theta\|_2^2 \quad (10)$$

θ is the model parameters. Experiments show that the performance improves after adding L_2 regularization. We train three models with different news grouping methods: time, topic and category, and we call them BHAM-Time, BHAM-Topic, BHAM-Category, respectively.

4 Experiment

4.1 Dataset

The experiment dataset is accessed from the professional finance news providers Reuters[2]. We collect forex trade data of four major currency pairs (USD-EUR, USD-JPY, USD-RMB, USD-GBP) from 2013 to 2017. We collect the open/close/high/low trade price for each trade minute. As for the finance news data, we collect all the English news happened in trade time released by Reuters and match the news with target currency pairs according to news region. For example, we match USD-EUR with news related to

US, Europe or both of them. The raw data contains both news headline and body, and we utilize the headline only since the headline contains the most valuable information and has less noise. The forex movement label f is decided by the comparison of prediction time price and the input window ending price. We design the symbol USD-EUR(20-10) to represent the prediction for the USD-EUR exchange rate with 20 minutes input time and 10 minutes prediction delay. To access more data for training, we overlap the input time of samples. For example, when overlap-rate is 50%, two consecutive samples' input time will be 8:00-8:20 am and 8:10-8:30 am. Then the data samples will be twice as large as no overlap condition (In the USD-EUR(20-10) dataset, the number of samples will increase from 31k to 62k). We reserve 5k samples for developing and 5k samples for testing. All the rest of samples are applied for training.

4.2 Experiment Setting

We choose the pytorch-pretrained-BERT[3] as BERT implement and choose the bert-base-uncased version in which there are 12 layers, 768 hidden states and 12 attention heads in the transformer. We truncate the BERT input to 256 tokens and fine-tune the BERT parameters during training. We adopt the Adam (Kingma and Ba, 2014) optimizer with the initial learning rate of 0.001. We apply the dropout (Srivastava et al., 2014) regularization with the dropout probability of 0.2 to reduce over-fitting. The batch size is 32. The training epoch is 60 with early stop. The weight of L_2 regularization is 0.015. The learning rate begins to decay after 10 epoch. The overlap rate of data samples is 50%, and the number of selected news in each group is 3. When splitting the dataset, we guarantee that the samples in train set are previous to samples in valid set and test set to avoid the possible information leakage. We tune the hyper-parameters on the development set and test model on the test set. The forex prediction is conducted as a binary classification task (up or down). The evaluation metrics are macro-F1 and Matthews Correlation Coefficient (**MCC**). MCC is often reported in stock movement forecast (Xu and Cohen, 2018; Ding et al., 2016) because it can overcome the data imbalance issue.

---

5 Results and Analysis

5.1 Comparison with Baselines

Here, we introduce the baselines in this work. Since there are few existing works, we modify two advanced models from stock prediction field which adopt multi-news as input for this task. Besides, we design some ablation variations of the proposed model to check the effects of different modules. The baselines are shown below:

- **NoNews:** This method considers the forex trade data only and use a 3-layer perceptron (the setting is same as full model) to encode the trade data and make prediction. This is a baseline to check the improvement by adding text information.

- **SVM:** This method chooses the support vector machine to predict the result based on the feature vectors extracted by the method introduced in (Seifollahi and Shajari, 2019).

- **HAN:** This method is proposed in (Hu et al., 2018) for stock movement prediction. It includes a hybrid attention mechanism and Gated Recurrent Unit to combine multi-day's stock news to predict movement. We use every 5 minutes instead of each day as time unit for this method and the StockNet method because there is too much news for forex trading and the experiments show that the latest news has the most influence.

- **StockNet:** This method is proposed in (Xu and Cohen, 2018). It treats the prediction task as a generation task and designs a modified variational auto encoder to process multi-days' tweets to predict stock movement.

- **NoGroup:** This method does not group news and select key news directly from all news.

- **NoConnect:** This method does not connect news in the same group. Instead, it gets the representation for each news independently using BERT. This method groups news by category.

- **LSTM+Attention:** This method uses the bi-directional LSTM and self-attention to replace the BERT as text encoder. The number of LSTM hidden states is 256, and the hidden-layer is 3. This method groups news by category.

As shown in Table 1, all the three proposed

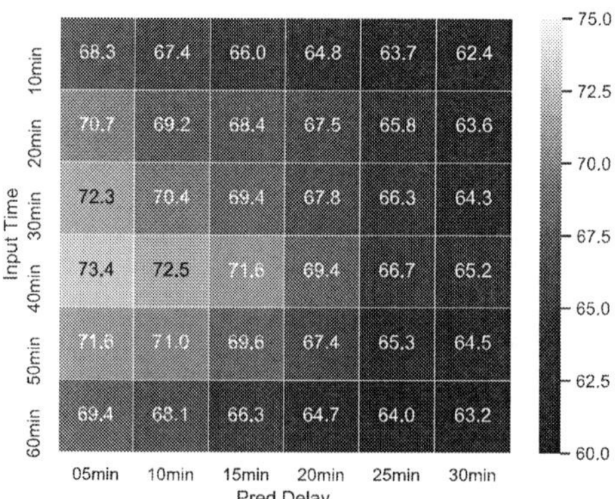

Figure 4: The BHAM-Category model's performances (macro-F1%) on USD-JPY pair under different conditions of input time and prediction delay. The dark colour means low performance and light colour means high performance.

methods perform well, and both BHAM-Topic and BHAM-Category methods outperform all the baselines. The BHAM-Category performs best among these methods, which shows that the semantic information of finance news is mostly aggregated by category. All the methods get improved after introducing the text information, which proves the related finance news is helpful for the prediction. The performance of NoGroup method decreases by a large margin compared to BHAM-Category, which demonstrates that the hierarchical structure works well. Without hierarchical structure, selecting essential news directly from all news has more noise and requires the model to have a stronger fitting ability for a longer paragraph. After removing the news connection, the performance of NoConnect method drops sharply compared to BHAM-Category. Accessing the news representation from the connected paragraph helps the news representation realize the context information in the group. The LSTM+Attention method performs worse than the BERT-based method, which proves that BERT has stronger power of sentence encoding. The two methods borrowed from stock movement prediction are designed to consider all news's information, but the forex related news is redundant, which can explain the poor performance of these two methods.

5.2 Effect of Time Parameters

In this section, we analyze the influence of two crucial time parameters on model performance, which are input time and predic-

	USD-EUR		USD-JPY		USD-RMB		USD-GBP	
Method	F1	MCC	F1	MCC	F1	MCC	F1	MCC
NoNews	63.0	0.266	64.8	0.295	65.4	0.304	64.7	0.301
SVM	64.8	0.297	65.7	0.314	66.2	0.324	65.1	0.310
HAN	65.2	0.305	67.0	0.341	66.7	0.334	66.9	0.346
StockNet	65.4	0.309	66.8	0.336	67.2	0.343	66.5	0.339
NoGroup	66.7	0.335	67.5	0.350	68.0	0.361	68.3	0.375
NoConnect	68.8	0.377	70.9	0.418	69.6	0.392	68.7	0.383
LSTM+Attention	69.8	0.397	71.2	0.422	71.8	0.434	69.7	0.403
BHAM-Time	70.7	0.414	70.5	0.409	71.4	0.426	69.2	0.392
BHAM-Topic	71.8	0.436	72.6	0.451	72.3	0.445	71.3	0.435
BHAM-Category	**72.5**	**0.450**	**73.4**	**0.466**	**73.5**	**0.468**	**71.6**	**0.441**

Table 1: Results of baselines and proposed methods on the test set (input time window is 40 minutes, and prediction delay is 5 minutes, we observe similar result in other time settings). All the experiment results have proven significant with $p < 0.05$ by student t-test.

tion delay. We choose the input time $\in \{10, 20, 30, 40, 50, 60\}$ (minutes), the prediction delay $\in \{5, 10, 15, 20, 25, 30\}$ (minutes) and experiment all combinations. We take the USD-JPY for example to analyze the time effect of forex trading, and we observe similar results in other currency pairs. The Figure 4 shows BHAM-Category model's performances (macro-F1%) on USD-JPY pair under different combinations of input time and prediction delay. We can observe that with the increase of input time from 10 minutes to 40 minutes, the model performance improves too. However, when we increase the input time continuously, the model performance begins to decrease. Too less text is not enough to support the prediction, but too many texts may bring much noise. The ideal input time is around 40 minutes. Besides, at all input time conditions, the model's performances decline with the increase of prediction delay because events happened in the prediction delay time may also influence the forex movement. We can also conclude that forex movement pays more attention to the latest news because when masking the latest news input (such as USD-JPY(40-05) and USD-JPY(30-15), the latter one can be seen as the former one masking the lastest 10 minutes input), the model performance declines obviously at almost all conditions.

5.3 Influence of News Attributes

In this section, we analyze the influence of finance news's attributes (category and region) on prediction results and summarize the influence patterns for different currency pairs. We conduct the experiments based on BHAM-Category.

5.3.1 Effect of News Category

The forex trading data's attention weights over news categories are calculated by Equation 6. We sum up all the attention weights of test samples and calculate the proportions each category contributes. As shown in Figure 5, we display the influence patterns of news category for different currency pairs. We observe that there are obvious differences among currency pairs. USD-EUR trading pays more attention to the Business Sectors and Politics/International Affairs news. USD-JPY trading is mostly influenced by Business Sectors and Science/Technology news. Politics/International Affairs news has the most significant impact on USD-RMB trading and Business Commodities news effects USD-GBP trading most. The summarized influence patterns can serve as decision-making reference for forex traders when facing news from various categories.

5.3.2 Effect of News Region

The trading data's attention weight for selected news att_{ij} is calculated by the following formula:

$$att_{ij} = att_i * s_j^i \qquad (11)$$

Where att_i is the trade data's attention on the i-th category in Equation 6 and s_j^i in Equation 4 is the weight of selected news in group. We sum up all the selected news's attention according to their regions and access the region influence weight. The results are shown in Figure 6. For each currency pair, the news are divided into three classes: news related to region A only, news related to region B only and news related to both region A and B. And we observe that the news related to both region A and B has the least influence on all currency

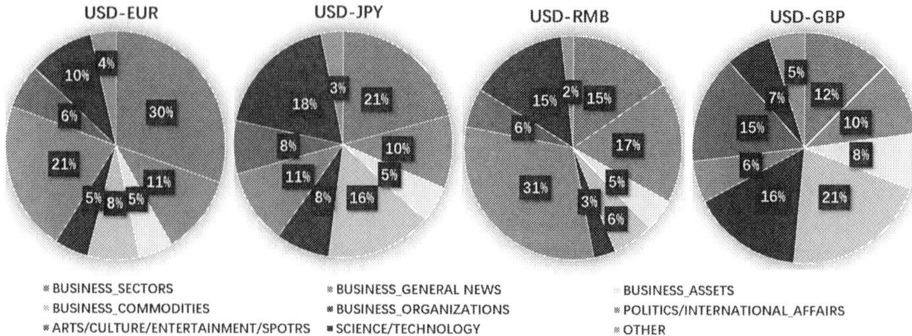

Figure 5: The attention distributions over categories for different currency pairs.

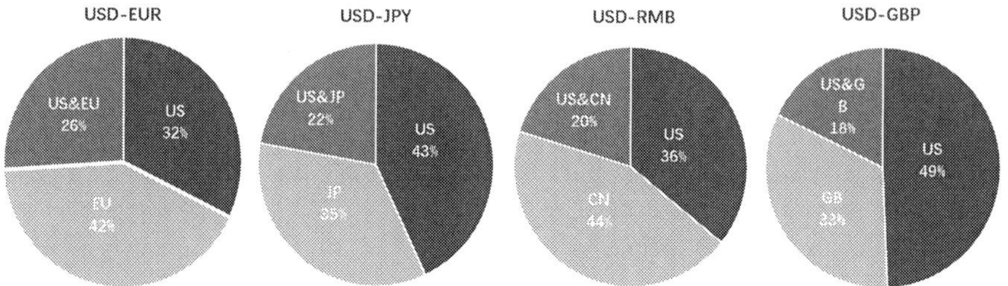

Figure 6: The attention distributions over regions for different currency pairs.

	USD-EUR	USD-JPY	USD-RMB	USD-GBP
1	67.6	68.8	69.3	67.3
2	71.4	73.1	72.2	70.8
3	**72.5**	**73.4**	**73.5**	**71.6**
4	72.2	72.8	73.1	70.7
5	70.8	70.3	71.9	68.4
∞	64.1	64.5	65.7	63.6

Table 2: Impact of selection number in each group in BHAM-Category. ∞ means keeping all news. The results have proven statistic significant.

pairs. News related to the US has the largest influence weight on USD-JPY and USD-GBP trading. Yet news related to China/Europe has a larger influence weight than news related to US in USD-RMB/USD-EUP trading. We can intuitively observe the influence weights of different regions for forex trading, which is helpful for the analysis and forecast of forex movement.

5.4 Impact of Selection Number

The selection number in each group is an essential hyper-parameter to control the amount of extracted information. As shown in Table 2, the BHAM-Category performs best when the selection number is 3 in all currency pairs. When the selection number is small (1,2), the model is too strict so that some crucial information will be missed. When the selection number is large (4,5), some less influential news will be selected and interfere model's decision. When we keep all news

in the group, the model's performance declines by a large margin. This experiment demonstrates that the selection mechanism plays an important role in the proposed model.

6 Conclusion

In this work, we propose a BERT-based Hierarchical Aggregation Model to summarize a large amount of finance news for forex movement prediction. Experiments show that our model outperforms all the baselines by a large margin, which proves the effectiveness of the proposed framework. We design three grouping news methods: time, topic and category and experiments show that the category-based method performs best, which shows that the semantic information of forex related news is mostly aggregated by category. Experiments about time effect prove that the proper input time is about 40 minutes and the prediction accuracy declines with the increase of prediction delay. Besides, we analyze the influence of news attributes on forex trading and observe some interesting conclusions: Business Sectors news has the most influence on USD-EUR trading and Politics/International Affairs news effects USD-RMB trading most. Besides, both USD-JPY trading and USD-GBP trading pay most attention to news from US. All these influence patterns can help forex traders handle different news more wisely and make better decisions.

To our knowledge, this is the first work to utilize the advanced NLP pre-train technology in the enormous forex market and the results show the potential of this research area. Promising future studies may include designing more suitable grouping methods or combining news grouping and market predicting in an end2end model.

7 Acknowledgement

This work is supported by a Research Grant from Mizuho Securities Co., Ltd. Mizuho Securities also provide experiment data and valuable domain experts suggestions.

References

Bernardo Jubert de Almeida, Rui Ferreira Neves, and Nuno Horta. 2018. Combining support vector machine with genetic algorithms to optimize investments in forex markets with high leverage. *Applied Soft Computing*, 64:596–613.

Hana Alostad and Hasan Davulcu. 2017. Directional prediction of stock prices using breaking news on twitter. *Web Intelligence*, 15(1):1–17.

Stefano Baccianella, Andrea Esuli, and Fabrizio Sebastiani. 2010. Sentiwordnet 3.0: an enhanced lexical resource for sentiment analysis and opinion mining. In *Lrec*, volume 10, pages 2200–2204.

Amer Bakhach, Edward PK Tsang, and Hamid Jalalian. 2016. Forecasting directional changes in the fx markets. In *2016 IEEE Symposium Series on Computational Intelligence (SSCI)*, pages 1–8. IEEE.

João Carapuço, Rui Neves, and Nuno Horta. 2018. Reinforcement learning applied to forex trading. *Applied Soft Computing*, 73:783–794.

Antonio V Contreras, Antonio Llanes, Alberto Pérez-Bernabeu, Sergio Navarro, Horacio Pérez-Sánchez, Jose J López-Espín, and José M Cecilia. 2018. Enmx: An elastic network model to predict the forex market evolution. *Simulation Modelling Practice and Theory*, 86:1–10.

Jacob Devlin, Ming-Wei Chang, Kenton Lee, and Kristina Toutanova. 2018. Bert: Pre-training of deep bidirectional transformers for language understanding. *arXiv preprint arXiv:1810.04805*.

Xiao Ding, Yue Zhang, Ting Liu, and Junwen Duan. 2016. Knowledge-driven event embedding for stock prediction. In *COLING 2016, 26th International Conference on Computational Linguistics, Proceedings of the Conference: Technical Papers, December 11-16, 2016, Osaka, Japan*, pages 2133–2142.

Junwen Duan, Yue Zhang, Xiao Ding, Ching-Yun Chang, and Ting Liu. 2018. Learning target-specific representations of financial news documents for cumulative abnormal return prediction. In *Proceedings of the 27th International Conference on Computational Linguistics, COLING 2018, Santa Fe, New Mexico, USA, August 20-26, 2018*, pages 2823–2833.

Brendan J Frey and Delbert Dueck. 2007. Clustering by passing messages between data points. *science*, 315(5814):972–976.

Ziniu Hu, Weiqing Liu, Jiang Bian, Xuanzhe Liu, and Tie-Yan Liu. 2018. Listening to chaotic whispers: A deep learning framework for news-oriented stock trend prediction. In *Proceedings of the Eleventh ACM International Conference on Web Search and Data Mining, WSDM 2018, Marina Del Rey, CA, USA, February 5-9, 2018*, pages 261–269.

Diederik P. Kingma and Jimmy Ba. 2014. Adam: A method for stochastic optimization. *CoRR*, abs/1412.6980.

Qing Li, LiLing Jiang, Ping Li, and Hsinchun Chen. 2015. Tensor-based learning for predicting stock movements. In *Proceedings of the Twenty-Ninth AAAI Conference on Artificial Intelligence, January 25-30, 2015, Austin, Texas, USA.*, pages 1784–1790.

Yang Liu. 2019. Fine-tune bert for extractive summarization.

George A Miller. 1995. Wordnet: a lexical database for english. *Communications of the ACM*, 38(11):39–41.

Lili Mou, Rui Men, Ge Li, Yan Xu, Lu Zhang, Rui Yan, and Zhi Jin. 2016. Natural language inference by tree-based convolution and heuristic matching. In *Proceedings of the 54th Annual Meeting of the Association for Computational Linguistics, ACL 2016, August 7-12, 2016, Berlin, Germany, Volume 2: Short Papers*.

Arman Khadjeh Nassirtoussi, Saeed Aghabozorgi, Teh Ying Wah, and David Chek Ling Ngo. 2015. Text mining of news-headlines for forex market prediction: A multi-layer dimension reduction algorithm with semantics and sentiment. *Expert Systems with Applications*, 42(1):306–324.

Lina Ni, Yujie Li, Xiao Wang, Jinquan Zhang, Jiguo Yu, and Chengming Qi. 2019. Forecasting of forex time series data based on deep learning. *Procedia computer science*, 147:647–652.

Dadabada Pradeepkumar and Vadlamani Ravi. 2016. Forex rate prediction using chaos and quantile regression random forest. In *2016 3rd International Conference on Recent Advances in Information Technology (RAIT)*, pages 517–522. IEEE.

Sasika Roledene, Lakna Ariyathilaka, Nadun Liyanage, Prasad Lakmal, and Jeewanee Bamunusinghe. 2016. Genibux-event based intelligent forex trading strategy enhancer. In *2016 IEEE International Conference on Information and Automation for Sustainability (ICIAfS)*, pages 1–6. IEEE.

Saeed Seifollahi and Mehdi Shajari. 2019. Word sense disambiguation application in sentiment analysis of news headlines: an applied approach to forex market prediction. *Journal of Intelligent Information Systems*, 52(1):57–83.

Hua Shen and Xun Liang. 2016. A time series forecasting model based on deep learning integrated algorithm with stacked autoencoders and svr for fx prediction. In *International Conference on Artificial Neural Networks*, pages 326–335. Springer.

Jianfeng Si, Arjun Mukherjee, Bing Liu, Sinno Jialin Pan, Qing Li, and Huayi Li. 2014. Exploiting social relations and sentiment for stock prediction. In *Proceedings of the 2014 Conference on Empirical Methods in Natural Language Processing, EMNLP 2014, October 25-29, 2014, Doha, Qatar, A meeting of SIGDAT, a Special Interest Group of the ACL*, pages 1139–1145.

Nitish Srivastava, Geoffrey E. Hinton, Alex Krizhevsky, Ilya Sutskever, and Ruslan Salakhutdinov. 2014. Dropout: a simple way to prevent neural networks from overfitting. *Journal of Machine Learning Research*, 15(1):1929–1958.

Nadine Strauß, Rens Vliegenthart, and Piet Verhoeven. 2018. Intraday news trading: The reciprocal relationships between the stock market and economic news. *Communication Research*, 45(7):1054–1077.

Chi Sun, Luyao Huang, and Xipeng Qiu. 2019. Utilizing bert for aspect-based sentiment analysis via constructing auxiliary sentence. *arXiv preprint arXiv:1903.09588*.

Yun-Cheng Tsai, Jun-Hao Chen, and Jun-Jie Wang. 2018. Predict forex trend via convolutional neural networks. *Journal of Intelligent Systems*.

Mrs Remya Vijayan and Mrs MA Potey. 2016. Improved accuracy of forex intraday trend prediction through text mining of news headlines using j48. *International Journal of Advanced Research in Computer Engineering & Technology (IJARCET)*, 5(6).

Wei Wang, Chen Wu, and Ming Yan. 2018. Multigranularity hierarchical attention fusion networks for reading comprehension and question answering. In *Proceedings of the 56th Annual Meeting of the Association for Computational Linguistics, ACL 2018, Melbourne, Australia, July 15-20, 2018, Volume 1: Long Papers*, pages 1705–1714.

NR Weeraddana, ATP Silva, and PWDC Jayathilake. 2018. Detection of black regions in the forex market by analyzing high-frequency intraday data. In *2018 18th International Conference on Advances in ICT for Emerging Regions (ICTer)*, pages 384–391. IEEE.

Hu Xu, Bing Liu, Lei Shu, and Philip S Yu. 2019. Bert post-training for review reading comprehension and aspect-based sentiment analysis. *arXiv preprint arXiv:1904.02232*.

Yumo Xu and Shay B. Cohen. 2018. Stock movement prediction from tweets and historical prices. In *Proceedings of the 56th Annual Meeting of the Association for Computational Linguistics, ACL 2018, Melbourne, Australia, July 15-20, 2018, Volume 1: Long Papers*, pages 1970–1979.

Yoke Leng Yong, Yunli Lee, Xiaowei Gu, Plamen P Angelov, David Chek Ling Ngo, and Elnaz Shafipour. 2018. Foreign currency exchange rate prediction using neuro-fuzzy systems. *Procedia computer science*, 144:232–238.

Complaint Analysis and Classification for Economic and Food Safety

João Filgueiras[*], Luís Barbosa[*], Gil Rocha[*], Henrique Lopes Cardoso[*], Luís Paulo Reis[*],
João Pedro Machado[+], Ana Maria Oliveira[+]

[*]Laboratório de Inteligência Artificial e Ciência de Computadores (LIACC)
Faculdade de Engenharia da Universidade do Porto
Rua Dr. Roberto Frias, s/n, 4200-465 Porto, Portugal
[+]Autoridade de Segurança Alimentar e Económica (ASAE),
Rua Rodrigo da Fonseca, 73, 1269-274 Lisboa, Portugal
{filgueiras, up201405729, gil.rocha, hlc, lpreis}@fe.up.pt
{jpmachado, amoliveira}@asae.pt

Abstract

Governmental institutions are employing artificial intelligence techniques to deal with their specific problems and exploit their huge amounts of both structured and unstructured information. In particular, natural language processing and machine learning techniques are being used to process citizen feedback. In this paper, we report on the use of such techniques for analyzing and classifying complaints, in the context of the Portuguese Economic and Food Safety Authority. Grounded in its operational process, we address three different classification problems: target economic activity, implied infraction severity level, and institutional competence. We show promising results obtained using feature-based approaches and traditional classifiers, with accuracy scores above 70%, and analyze the shortcomings of our current results and avenues for further improvement, taking into account the intended use of our classifiers in helping human officers to cope with thousands of yearly complaints.

1 Introduction

Artificial intelligence (AI) techniques are nowadays widespread in virtually every sector of human activity. Not only the private sector but also public administration institutions and governments are looking into ways of taking advantage of AI to deal with their specific problems and exploit their substantial amounts of both structured and unstructured information. Natural language processing (NLP) techniques are being employed in this regard to handle text available in the web (such as in social networks or newswires) and, most importantly, written forms of direct interaction between citizens and governmental institutions (Eggers, 2019).

Several governmental institutions provide public services electronically. Moreover, such institutions are responsible for processing citizen feedback (such as requests or complaints), often materialized through email or contact forms in so-called virtual counters. The amount of such contacts can become intractable in a short period of time, depending on the size of the country/administrative region. Based on such information, NLP techniques can be used to improve public services (Kowalski et al., 2019).

This paper focuses on the needs of the Portuguese Economic and Food Safety Authority (ASAE)[1], a national administrative authority specialized in the context of food safety and economic surveillance, responsible for monitoring and enforcing regulatory legislation. One of the main inputs of this institution is comprised of citizen complaints on the activity of economic agents, with more than twenty thousand complaints being received annually. Usually, more than 30% of these are found not to be in the jurisdiction of this authority; the remaining are sent to specific operational units. The use of human labor to analyze and properly handle these complaints is a bottleneck, bringing the need to automate this process to the extent possible. Doing it effectively is hindered by the fact that contact forms typically include free-form text fields, bringing high variability to the quality of the content written by citizens (which can be considered as user-generated content (Momeni et al., 2015)).

In this paper we present an analysis of a rich dataset containing 150,700 complaints related to food safety and economic surveillance. We also present machine learning-based classifiers that perform accurately for three key dimensions that are especially important for ASAE. Initial experiments using Deep Learning architectures are also reported. To the best of our knowledge, this is

---

[1]http://www.asae.gov.pt/welcome-to-website-asae.aspx

Proceedings of the Second Workshop on Economics and Natural Language Processing, pages 51–60
Hong Kong, November 4. ©2019 Association for Computational Linguistics

the first study of its kind regarding food safety and economic surveillance complaints for the Portuguese language.

In Section 2, we start by providing a short analysis of related work. Section 3 explains the overall complaint processing steps considered and provides an exploratory data analysis. Section 4 explains the main choices regarding preprocessing and feature extraction, that are common to all addressed classification tasks, whose details and experimental results are further developed in Sections 5, 6 and 7. Section 8 concludes the paper and points to directions for future work.

2 Related Work

Works on analyzing user-generated content mostly study social media data (Batrinca and Treleaven, 2015), focusing on tasks such as sentiment analysis (Eshleman and Yang, 2014; Forte and Brazdil, 2016) and opinion mining (Petz et al., 2013), or predicting the usefulness of product reviews (Diaz and Ng, 2018). For instance, Forte and Brazdil (2016) focus on sentiment polarity of Portuguese comments from the customer service department of a major Portuguese telecommunications company and use a lexicon-based approach enriched with domain-specific terms, formulating specific rules for negation and amplifiers.

Literature on non-social media complaint analysis is considerably more scarce, mainly due to the fact that such data is typically not publicly available. Even so, the problem has received significant attention from the NLP community, as a recent task on consumer feedback analysis shows (Liu et al., 2017). Given the different kinds of analysis one may want to undertake, however, the task concentrates on a single goal: to distinguish between comment, request, bug, complaint, and meaningless. In our work, we need to further analyze the contents of complaints, with a finer granularity.

Ordenes et al. (2014) propose a framework for analyzing customer experience feedback, using a linguistics-based model. This approach explores the identification of activities, resources and context, so as to automatically distinguish compliments from complaints, regarding different aspects of customer feedback. The work focuses on a single activity domain and, in the end, aims at obtaining a refined sentiment analysis model. In our work, we avoid entering into a labor-intensive annotation process of domain-specific data and fo-

cus on cross-domain classification tasks that help in complaint processing.

Traditional approaches to text categorization employ feature-based sparse models, using bag-of-words and Term Frequency-Inverse Document Frequency (TF-IDF) encoding. In the context of insurance complaint handling, Dong and Wang (2015) make use of synonyms and Chi-square statistics to reduce the dimensionality of the feature space. More recent techniques, such as word embeddings (Mikolov et al., 2013) and recurrent neural networks (RNNs) (Elman, 1990), have also been used in complaint classification. Assawinjaipetch et al. (2016) employ these methods to classify complaints of a single company into one of nine classes, related to the specific aspect that is being criticized.

Given the noisy nature of user-generated content, dealing with complaints as a multi-label classification problem can be effective, even when the original problem is single-labeled. Ranking algorithms (Li, 2014; Momeni et al., 2015) are a promising approach in this regard, providing a set of predictions sorted by confidence. These techniques have been applied in complaint analysis by Fauzan and Khodra (2014), although with modest results.

Kalyoncu et al. (2018) approach customer complaint analysis from a topic modeling perspective, using techniques such as Latent Dirichlet Allocation (LDA) (Blei et al., 2003). This work is not so much focused on automatically processing complaints, but instead on providing a visualization tool for mobile network operators.

3 Complaint Data

Among several other responsibilities pertaining to economic and food safety, ASAE, the Portuguese Economic and Food Safety Authority, is also responsible for handling consumer complaints. These complaints can be submitted by any citizen, either through a website form submission (including a free-form text field) or directly by email. Once a complaint is received, it must be handled by an officer, who is responsible for extracting all relevant information and filling it as part of a more structured complaint format in the back-end. This structured complaint will then be used to decide if and when it should be investigated.

3.1 Key Dimensions

There are a number of fields that are part of the final complaint structure before it is acted upon. More specifically, and in addition to context information such as names and addresses of the entities involved, there are three key dimensions.

The first is the type of *economic activity* related to the complaint. In total 11 categories can be assigned to a complaint ranging, for example, from online sales to restaurants. The type of activity is an important aspect for ASAE coordination, as a number of its operations are dedicated to specific activities within a long-term predefined strategic plan.

The second key dimension is *infraction severity*. This dimension concerns the infractions implied by the complaint. Each infraction can be considered an administrative infringement, a crime or a simple consumer conflict. Understanding the severity of infractions allows ASAE to prioritize investigating more serious and potentially harmful complaint targets.

Finally, the third key dimension is *competence*. This dimension essentially indicates whether a complaint refers to an event that is within ASAE jurisdiction, or if it should be treated by a different judicial or governmental entity. This distinction is important because ASAE should not investigate complaints outside its jurisdiction and should also forward the complaint to the competent authority.

3.2 Exploratory Data Analysis

The dataset used for the experiments presented in this work consists of 150,700 complaints, written in Portuguese, received by ASAE over the course of 11 years, starting in 2008 and ending in 2018. In addition to the textual contents of each complaint, the dataset contains all annotations performed by ASAE officers. This allows for a detailed analysis of the complaints received by the public entity, which falls outside the scope of this paper but is summarized in this section.

Table 1 shows the distribution for economic activities. It is fairly unbalanced, with a majority class taking 32.07% of all examples, and the most underrepresented class having only 0.02%. The top 3 classes represent in total 72% of the dataset. Class Z is a special case because it signals that no economic activity has been perceived in the complaint. Only 146,847 complaints are considered for this dimension because the remaining 3,853 do

not have a valid economic activity label, i. e., differently from class Z examples which indicate that no economic activity was identified, these examples do not have a classification label in terms of economic activity.

Each complaint can include several different infraction indications, which in turn means one complaint can contain infractions of varying severity. In order to simplify the problem, we decided to focus on the highest infraction severity implied by each complaint. This makes prioritization easier – a complaint indicating crime is more severe than a complaint pointing only to administrative infringements – but also makes classification fuzzier due to the overlap between crimes and administrative infringements in some cases. The distribution among the resulting three classes is shown in Table 2.

Table 3 shows the data distribution based on the competence label. While the original dataset provides a list of entities that should ultimately handle each complaint, the focus of the experiments reported in this paper is solely to determine whether ASAE is one of them.

Class	# compl	%
I - Primary Production	572	0.39
II - Industry	4,214	2.87
III - Restoration	47,098	32.07
IV - Wholesalers	631	0.43
V - Retail	13,904	9.47
VI - Direct selling	27	0.02
VII - Distance selling	4,760	3.24
VIII - Production & Trade	14,236	9.69
IX - Service Providers	35,737	24.34
X - Safety & Environment	1,905	1.30
Z - No activity identified	23,763	16.18
Total	146,847	100.00

Table 1: Economic activity class distribution

Class	# compl	%
Crime	8,086	5.37
Admin. infringement	69,012	45.79
Other	73,602	48.84
Total	150,700	100.00

Table 2: Infraction severity class distribution

The complaints are evenly distributed across time, roughly 14,000 per year, with a slight increase towards the last 5 years. A geographical

Class	# compl	%
ASAE and others	94,140	62.47
Other	56,560	37.53
Total	150,700	100.00

Table 3: Competence class distribution (binary setting)

analysis reveals that more densely populated areas generate more complaints, as expected.

A majority of 63% complaints are received via the ASAE website. The complaint form is mostly free-text but it does specifically request the author to identify himself by providing his name, address, phone number and email address. The author is also requested to identify the entity targeted by the complaint using the same information. Unfortunately, not every complaint provides enough context or information to successfully determine the target entity, making it impossible to investigate.

4 Experimental Setup

In order to implement machine learning classifiers based on the textual contents of each complaint, and given their user-generated content nature, a previous preprocessing step was necessary. Based on an earlier work that tackled economic activity prediction on a smaller sample of this dataset (Barbosa et al., 2019), the dataset was preprocessed using the Natural Language Toolkit (NLTK) (Bird et al., 2009) to perform tokenization, lemmatization and remove stop words from Portuguese text. Furthermore, from among the different feature-based representations explored by Barbosa et al. (2019), a TF-IDF weighted vector was found to be the most effective method of representing each document. TF-IDF outperformed fastText-based (Joulin et al., 2016) and BERT-based (Devlin et al., 2018) representations, using traditional machine learning approaches, specifically Support Vector Machines (SVM) (Cortes and Vapnik, 1995).

For all experiments reported in this paper, the split between training and test sets was performed bearing in mind that the processes used by ASAE have suffered small changes over the last decade and that the ultimate goal is to help officers perform their work more efficiently when handling complaints nowadays. As such, the test set used in these experiments has been drawn from the last 5 years of data only. This also ensures the results for the task of economic activity prediction reported in this paper can be compared to results from ear-

lier work (Barbosa et al., 2019), which were obtained using the same test set. A total of roughly 25,000 examples make up this test set, 16% of all available data. For each task, a different stratified splitting was performed, to ensure that the resulting test sets followed the target distribution.

The following classifiers were employed: Naïve Bayes (NB) (Manning et al., 2008), K-Neighbors (Altman, 1992), SVM, Stochastic Gradient Descent (SGD) (Zhang, 2004), Decision Tree Classifier (Quinlan, 1986), Randomized Decision Trees (also know as extra-trees)(Geurts et al., 2006), Random Forests (Breiman, 2001), and Bagging Classifier (Breiman, 1996). For all ensemble models (i.e. Randomized Decision Trees, Random Forests, and Bagging Classifier), Decision Trees are used as weak classifiers with default parameters. For reference, we also report the scores of a random classifier that generates predictions based only on the training set label distribution (dubbed "Random (stratified)").

The scikit-learn library (Pedregosa et al., 2011) was used to implement bag-of-words and TF-IDF encoding, train-test set stratified splitting and all classifiers, unless otherwise stated.

As evaluation metric, we focused on the accuracy score (Acc), because, for the application scenario at ASAE, we aim to classify the complaints as accurately as possible. However, given the unbalanced nature of the label distribution, we also report Macro-F1 scores, which provide an estimate on how good the classifiers are across different labels, without taking into account label imbalance.

5 Economic Activity Prediction

One of the first steps needed to analyze a complaint concerns the identification of the targeted economic activity, from those shown in Table 1. We model this as a classification problem with 11 classes. Given the relatively high number of classes, we also look at the performance of each classifier considering its ranked output. This approach is aligned with the potential usage of the classifier, which is meant to help humans analyze complaints by providing likely classification labels (as opposed to imposing a definitive one).

Table 4 summarizes the scores obtained for this task, where Acc@k and Macro-F1@k are accuracy and macro-F1 scores, respectively, when considering that the classifier has made a correct prediction if any of the k most confidently predicted classes (top-k) corresponds to the target label. Overall, the best classifier is a SVM with a linear kernel, achieving the highest accuracy and macro-F1 scores for every top-k, with the exception of top-3 accuracy, where SGD outperforms SVM by under 1%. Both SVM and SGD perform considerably better than any other alternatives, notably Random Forests. All classifiers significantly outperform the stratified random baseline.

5.1 Error Analysis

Based on the different accuracy and average macro-F1 scores obtained, we have decided to focus on SVM for the sake of error analysis. The SVM confusion matrix is shown in Table 5 and is complemented by the per-class precision and recall metrics displayed in Table 6.

The influence of majority classes III and IX is visible, while class Z (in which no economic activity is identified) seems to be the most ambiguous for the classifier, given also its high number of examples. In fact, class III has the highest recall, but also precision. Most other classes have good precision scores, while some of them suffer from low recall, namely: classes I, IV, and X. Class VI contains too few examples to be considered.

While inspecting some of the misclassified instances, a number of issues became apparent. Some examples comprise short text complaints, not providing enough information to classify their target economic activity. A small number of complaints are not written in Portuguese. Some complaint texts are followed by non-complaint-related content, sometimes in English. Some classes exhibit semantic overlap. For instance, class VIII (Production & Trade) overlaps with classes II (Industry) and V (Retail). That means that complaints labeled VII often contain words that are highly correlated with II and V. A non-negligible number of examples refer to previously submitted complaints, either to provide more data or to request information on their status. These cases do not contain the complaint itself, the same happening when a short text simply includes meta-data or points to an attached file. Finally, we were able to identify some complaints that have been misclassified by the human operator.

As mentioned previously, and plainly observable in Table 1, this classification problem is very imbalanced. In previous work (Barbosa et al., 2019), while considering a sample of the dataset with half the time window (and thus with approximately half the size, while maintaining a similar class distribution), we have tried employing both random undersampling and random oversampling (He and Garcia, 2009), in order to improve the overall classification performance and, more specifically, the performance on minority classes. However, such attempts did not succeed, consistently worsening results.

Because class Z is used to indicate that no activity has been identified and, for that reason, is highly diffuse, we have conducted a few experiments to try to find better approaches of dealing with this class. Removing class Z from the training subset, while assuming this class as the correct label in the absence of an above-threshold confidence in any class, did not bring satisfactory results, as no appropriate threshold could be found. Otherwise, assuming class Z as the correct label when it is one of the top-2 predicted classes also lowered scores significantly.

5.2 Deep Learning Approaches

As part of an effort to further improve the classification results on this task, that proved to be more challenging given the number of classes and their similarities, a shift was made from traditional feature-based approaches to word embeddings and deep neural network architectures (deep learning approaches). In particular, a number of experiments using long short-term memory neural networks (LSTM) (Hochreiter and Schmidhuber, 1997) were performed. While these results are preliminary, the best configuration of an LSTM-based classifier achieved an accuracy of 0.695 and a macro-F1 of 0.44. This particular configuration used a hidden layer of size 1024 and we retrain the embeddings with 300 dimensions that were initialized randomly. Adam (Kingma and Ba, 2014) was used for optimization and negative log-likelihood loss chosen as the cost function. Standard first choices were used for the remaining hyperparameters, including: learning rate of 0.001 (Kingma and Ba, 2014), dropout of 0.2 (Srivastava et al., 2014), and batch size of 32. Initial experiments focused on variations of these parameters: learning rates between 0.001 and 0.0001; dropout between 0.2 and 0.5. Runs with fixed or trainable embeddings and different hidden layer sizes (128 to 1024) were also attempted.

Classifier	Acc@1	Acc@2	Acc@3	Macro-F1@1	Macro-F1@2	Macro-F1@3
Random (stratified)	0.2035	0.3314	0.3704	0.09	0.16	0.23
Bernoulli NB	0.4554	0.6567	0.7998	0.16	0.28	0.37
Multinomial NB	0.4786	0.6049	0.7332	0.11	0.18	0.28
Complement NB	0.5922	0.7873	0.8944	0.29	0.48	0.61
K-Neighbors	0.2949	0.4701	0.6078	0.18	0.31	0.42
SVM (linear)	**0.7554**	**0.8792**	0.9320	**0.57**	**0.72**	**0.79**
SGD	0.7379	0.8739	**0.9404**	0.51	0.66	0.75
Decision Tree	0.5987	0.6985	0.7141	0.39	0.46	0.48
Extra Tree	0.4162	0.5265	0.5495	0.26	0.32	0.35
Random Forests	0.6247	0.7854	0.8807	0.37	0.50	0.59
Bagging	0.6617	0.8054	0.8709	0.44	0.56	0.64

Table 4: Economic activity prediction results

Predicted

	I	II	III	IV	V	VI	VII	VIII	IX	X	Z
I	**43**	5	4	0	11	0	0	4	4	0	17
II	0	**384**	127	6	61	0	1	15	30	0	78
III	0	68	**7,036**	2	89	0	5	40	209	4	205
IV	0	10	10	**26**	17	0	0	6	8	0	30
V	1	22	141	5	**1,845**	0	9	56	63	0	113
VI	0	0	0	0	0	**0**	0	1	0	0	0
VII	0	0	7	0	12	0	**864**	58	114	0	101
VIII	1	7	122	4	57	0	49	**1,502**	268	6	259
IX	1	9	379	4	35	0	53	166	**4,895**	6	380
X	0	4	22	1	11	0	13	62	83	**114**	56
Z	11	65	480	9	155	0	108	356	824	25	**1,388**

The row labels I–Z are grouped under the side heading **Actual**.

Table 5: Economic activity prediction confusion matrix using SVM (top-1)

The training process was allowed to run for a maximum of 20 epochs. However, for each epoch, the training process measured accuracy on a separate development set and kept the model that performed best. The neural network architectures were implemented using PyTorch (Paszke et al., 2017).

While the results are still far from the accuracy obtained using SVMs, 0.755, further experiments are planned using pre-trained embeddings, such as fastText and BERT, combined with different deep learning architectures, including convolutional neural networks (Dos Santos and Gatti, 2014) and attention mechanisms (Bahdanau et al., 2015; Yang et al., 2016).

6 Infraction Severity Prediction

The priority of a complaint is directly related to the infractions that emerge from the reported information. Instead of predicting infractions, however, we focus on their severity, in a three-layered framework (as shown in Table 2). As mentioned in Section 3, we decided to reduce the problem from a multi-label and multi-class setting to a single-label problem, where we identify the most severe type of infraction evidenced by the complaint: a crime or an administrative infringement.

The accuracy and macro-F1 scores obtained using different classifiers are shown in Table 7. Contrary to the results of predicting economic activity, SGD performs slightly better in terms of accuracy, while SVM still leads on macro-F1 score. Once again, both SVM and SGD outperform other classifiers. However, for this task the differences are not as pronounced, especially in relation to Bagging and to a lesser extent Random Forests. Every classifier outperforms the baseline.

6.1 Error Analysis

As before, we focus on SVM for the sake of error analysis, although SGD would also be a valid op-

	Precision	Recall
I	0.75	0.49
II	0.67	0.55
III	0.84	0.92
IV	0.46	0.24
V	0.80	0.82
VI	–	0.00
VII	0.78	0.75
VIII	0.66	0.66
IX	0.75	0.83
X	0.74	0.31
Z	0.53	0.41

Table 6: Economic activity prediction precision and recall per class (top-1)

Classifier	Acc	Macro-F1
Random (stratified)	0.4499	0.33
Bernoulli NB	0.5909	0.40
Multinomial NB	0.6731	0.46
Complement NB	0.6750	0.50
K-Neighbors	0.4859	0.36
SVM (linear)	0.7075	**0.66**
SGD	**0.7231**	0.64
Decision Tree	0.6242	0.56
Extra Tree	0.5709	0.47
Random Forests	0.6881	0.55
Bagging	0.6805	0.62

Table 7: Infraction severity prediction results

tion. By analyzing the confusion matrix shown in Table 8, it is possible to observe that class "Administrative infringement" and "Others" have a considerable number of cases where the prediction is swapped. Furthermore, several crime cases are being wrongly classified. A source of confusion between administrative infringements and crimes is their co-occurrence in some complaints of the original data (as mentioned in Section 3.2), and results from reducing the problem to a single-label setting.

		Predicted		
		Crime	Adm. infr.	Other
Actual	Crime	**579**	362	324
	Adm. infr.	95	**8,371**	3,089
	Other	153	2,984	**8,000**

Table 8: Infraction severity prediction confusion matrix using SVM

Although the accuracy and macro-F1 scores are not low, there is considerable room for improvement in this particular task. Taking into account the application of this classification model in food safety and economic surveillance, special attention should be given to false negatives of the "Crime" and "Administrative infringement" classes.

7 Competence Prediction

In practice, identifying the competent entity(ies) to handle a complaint is determined by the output of the previous two dimensions: economic activity and infractions. However, since we are not directly predicting infractions (but rather their severity), we have chosen to predict the competence directly from the complaint contents. As mentioned in Section 3.2, we decided to reduce the competence prediction problem to a binary classification setting (as per Table 3), where we identify whether ASAE is one of the institutions responsible to handle the complaint or not.

The accuracy and macro-F1 scores obtained using different classifiers are shown in Table 9. In consistence with the other tasks, SGD and SVM perform better than all remaining classifiers, with Bagging and Random Forests slightly behind. For this task, K-Neighbours and Multinomial NB are not particularly far from the baseline.

Classifier	Acc	Macro-F1
Random (stratified)	0.5308	0.50
Bernoulli NB	0.6866	0.65
Multinomial NB	0.6661	0.53
Complement NB	0.6929	0.60
K-Neighbors	0.5877	0.57
SVM (linear)	**0.7953**	**0.78**
SGD	0.7927	**0.78**
Decision Tree	0.7002	0.68
Extra Tree	0.6532	0.63
Random Forests	0.7477	0.70
Bagging	0.7440	0.73

Table 9: Competence prediction results

7.1 Error Analysis

SVM is again chosen for error analysis. Table 10 presents the confusion matrix for this task and shows there is a considerable amount of cases where the prediction is incorrect. As with the previous task, we are particularly interested in addressing false negatives of the ASAE class.

	Predicted	
	ASAE	Other
ASAE	**12,408**	2,243
Other	2,662	**6,644**

Table 10: Competence prediction confusion matrix using SVM

It should be noted that our results show that it is possible, to a large extent, to derive ASAE's competence directly from the complaint text (with a recall of 85%). Albeit this does not correspond to the current practice, it does comprise a promising shortcut to this task.

8 Conclusions

In this paper, we present our findings regarding the classification of complaints, written in the Portuguese language, along three key dimensions: economic activity, infraction severity and competence. Traditional machine learning and natural language processing approaches, such as bag-of-words with TF-IDF encoding and SVM models, provide fairly accurate classifiers for these tasks. Our preliminary work using Deep Learning approaches requires further investigation (*e.g.* exploring different architectures) and have yet to reach the same levels of performance.

This work can be integrated in an AI-powered web platform to help ASAE officers in their efforts to tackle the large amount of complaints received, not only by providing semi-automatic annotating capabilities but also for managing work prioritization. The classifiers, however, still reveal some limitations. In particular, for economic activity, the Z class – no discernible economic activity – is still a source of considerable confusion. Strategies to overcome this limitation have not been successful yet. For infraction severity, it would be important to achieve better results distinguishing crimes from other infractions, as these should receive the highest priority.

Additional work is planned to counter these limitations and strive for more accurate classifiers, in an effort to further improve the performance of the system. In particular, we are experimenting with different deep learning architectures, pre-trained word embeddings, and hyperparameter fine-tuning of the machine learning models.

Acknowledgments

This work is supported by project IA.SAE, funded by Fundação para a Ciência e a Tecnologia (FCT) through program INCoDe.2030. Gil Rocha is supported by a PhD scholarship from FCT (SFRH/BD/140125/2018).

References

N. S. Altman. 1992. An introduction to kernel and nearest-neighbor nonparametric regression. *The American Statistician*, 46(3):175–185.

Panuwat Assawinjaipetch, Kiyoaki Shirai, Virach Sornlertlamvanich, and Sanparith Marukata. 2016. Recurrent Neural Network with Word Embedding for Complaint Classification. In *Proceedings of the Third International Workshop on Worldwide Language Service Infrastructure and Second Workshop on Open Infrastructures and Analysis Frameworks for Human Language Technologies (WLSI/OIAF4HLT2016)*, pages 36–43, Osaka, Japan. The COLING 2016 Organizing Committee.

Dzmitry Bahdanau, Kyunghyun Cho, and Yoshua Bengio. 2015. Neural machine translation by jointly learning to align and translate. In *3rd International Conference on Learning Representations, ICLR 2015, San Diego, CA, USA, May 7-9, 2015, Conference Track Proceedings*.

Luís Barbosa, João Filgueiras, Gil Rocha, Henrique Lopes Cardoso, Luís Paulo Reis, João Pedro Machado, Ana Cristina Caldeira, and Ana Maria Oliveira. 2019. Automatic Identification of Economic Activities in Complaints. In *Statistical Language and Speech Processing, 7th International Conference, SLSP 2019, Ljubljana, Slovenia, October 1416, 2019, Proceedings*, volume 11816 of *LNAI*. Springer.

Bogdan Batrinca and Philip C. Treleaven. 2015. Social media analytics: a survey of techniques, tools and platforms. *AI & Society*, 30(1):89–116.

Steven Bird, Ewan Klein, and Edward Loper. 2009. *Natural Language Processing with Python*, 1st edition. O'Reilly Media, Inc.

David M. Blei, Andrew Y. Ng, and Michael I. Jordan. 2003. Latent Dirichlet Allocation. *Journal of Machine Learning Research*, 3:993–1022.

Leo Breiman. 1996. Bagging predictors. *Machine Learning*, 24(2):123–140.

Leo Breiman. 2001. Random forests. *Machine Learning*, 45(1):5–32.

Corinna Cortes and Vladimir Vapnik. 1995. Support-vector networks. *Machine Learning*, 20(3):273–297.

Jacob Devlin, Ming-Wei Chang, Kenton Lee, and Kristina Toutanova. 2018. Bert: Pre-training of deep bidirectional transformers for language understanding. *arXiv preprint arXiv:1810.04805*.

Gerardo Ocampo Diaz and Vincent Ng. 2018. Modeling and Prediction of Online Product Review Helpfulness: A Survey. In *Proceedings of the 56th Annual Meeting of the Association for Computational Linguistics*, pages 698–708.

Shuang Dong and Zhihong Wang. 2015. Evaluating Service Quality in Insurance Customer Complaint Handling throught Text Categorization. In *2015 Int. Conf. on Logistics, Informatics and Service Sciences (LISS)*, pages 1–5. IEEE.

Cicero Dos Santos and Maira Gatti. 2014. Deep convolutional neural networks for sentiment analysis of short texts. In *Proceedings of COLING 2014, the 25th International Conference on Computational Linguistics: Technical Papers*, pages 69–78.

William D. Eggers. 2019. Using AI to unleash the power of unstructured government data. *Deloitte Insights*.

Jeffrey L. Elman. 1990. Finding structure in time. *Cognitive Science*, 14(2):179–211.

Ryan M. Eshleman and Hui Yang. 2014. "Hey #311, Come Clean My Street!": A Spatio-temporal Sentiment Analysis of Twitter Data and 311 Civil Complaints. In *2014 IEEE Fourth International Conference on Big Data and Cloud Computing*, pages 477–484.

Ahmad Fauzan and Masayu Leylia Khodra. 2014. Automatic Multilabel Categorization using Learning to Rank Framework for Complaint Text on Bandung Government. In *2014 Int. Conf. of Advanced Informatics: Concept, Theory and Application (ICAICTA)*, pages 28–33. Institut Teknologi Bandung, IEEE.

Ana Catarina Forte and Pavel B. Brazdil. 2016. Determining the Level of Clients' Dissatisfaction from Their Commentaries. In *Computational Processing of the Portuguese Language - 12th Int. Conf., PROPOR 2016*, volume 9727 of *Lecture Notes in Computer Science*, pages 74–85. Springer.

Pierre Geurts, Damien Ernst, and Louis Wehenkel. 2006. Extremely randomized trees. *Machine Learning*, 63(1):3–42.

Haibo He and Edwardo A. Garcia. 2009. Learning from Imbalanced Data. *IEEE Trans. on Knowl. and Data Eng.*, 21(9):1263–1284.

Sepp Hochreiter and Jürgen Schmidhuber. 1997. Long short-term memory. *Neural Comput.*, 9(8):1735–1780.

Armand Joulin, Edouard Grave, Piotr Bojanowski, and Tomas Mikolov. 2016. Bag of tricks for efficient text classification. *arXiv preprint arXiv:1607.01759*.

Feyzullah Kalyoncu, Engin Zeydan, Ibrahim Onuralp Yigit, and Ahmet Yildirim. 2018. A Customer Complaint Analysis Tool for Mobile Network Operators. In *2018 IEEE/ACM Int. Conf. on Advances in Social Networks Analysis and Mining (ASONAM)*, pages 609–612. IEEE.

Diederik P Kingma and Jimmy Ba. 2014. Adam: A method for stochastic optimization. *arXiv preprint arXiv:1412.6980*.

Radoslaw Kowalski, Marc Esteve, and Slava Jankin Mikhaylov. 2019. Improving Public Services by Mining Citizen Feedback: An Application of Natural Language Processing. *EasyChair preprint 1103*.

Hang Li. 2014. *Learning to Rank for Information Retrieval and Natural Language Processing*, 2 edition. Synthesis Lectures on Human Language Technologies. Morgan & Claypool Publ., San Rafael, CA.

Chao-Hong Liu, Yasufumi Moriya, Alberto Poncelas, and Declan Groves. 2017. IJCNLP-2017 Task 4: Customer Feedback Analysis. In *Proceedings of the IJCNLP 2017, Shared Tasks*, pages 26–33, Taipei, Taiwan. Asian Federation of Natural Language Processing.

Christopher D. Manning, Prabhakar Raghavan, and Hinrich Schütze. 2008. *Introduction to Information Retrieval*. Cambridge University Press, New York, NY, USA.

Tomas Mikolov, Ilya Sutskever, Kai Chen, Greg S Corrado, and Jeff Dean. 2013. Distributed representations of words and phrases and their compositionality. In C. J. C. Burges, L. Bottou, M. Welling, Z. Ghahramani, and K. Q. Weinberger, editors, *Advances in Neural Information Processing Systems 26*, pages 3111–3119. Curran Associates, Inc.

Elaheh Momeni, Claire Cardie, and Nicholas Diakopoulos. 2015. A Survey on Assessment and Ranking Methodologies for User-Generated Content on the Web. *ACM Computing Surveys*, 48(3):41:1–41:49.

Francisco Villarroel Ordenes, Babis Theodoulidis, Jamie Burton, Thorsten Gruber, and Mohamed Zaki. 2014. Analyzing Customer Experience Feedback Using Text Mining: A Linguistics-Based Approach. *Journal of Service Research*, 17(3):278–295.

Adam Paszke, Sam Gross, Soumith Chintala, Gregory Chanan, Edward Yang, Zachary DeVito, Zeming Lin, Alban Desmaison, Luca Antiga, and Adam Lerer. 2017. Automatic differentiation in PyTorch. In *NIPS Autodiff Workshop: The Future of Gradient-based Machine Learning Software and Techniques*.

F. Pedregosa, G. Varoquaux, A. Gramfort, V. Michel, B. Thirion, O. Grisel, M. Blondel, P. Prettenhofer, R. Weiss, V. Dubourg, J. Vanderplas, A. Passos, D. Cournapeau, M. Brucher, M. Perrot, and E. Duchesnay. 2011. Scikit-learn: Machine learning in Python. *Journal of Machine Learning Research*, 12:2825–2830.

Gerald Petz, Michał Karpowicz, Harald Fürschuß, Andreas Auinger, Václav Stříteský, and Andreas Holzinger. 2013. Opinion Mining on the Web 2.0 – Characteristics of User Generated Content and Their Impacts. In *Human-Computer Interaction and Knowledge Discovery in Complex, Unstructured, Big Data*, pages 35–46. Springer.

J. R. Quinlan. 1986. Induction of decision trees. *Mach. Learn.*, 1(1):81–106.

Nitish Srivastava, Geoffrey Hinton, Alex Krizhevsky, Ilya Sutskever, and Ruslan Salakhutdinov. 2014. Dropout: A simple way to prevent neural networks from overfitting. *Journal of Machine Learning Research*, 15:1929–1958.

Zichao Yang, Diyi Yang, Chris Dyer, Xiaodong He, Alex Smola, and Eduard Hovy. 2016. Hierarchical attention networks for document classification. In *Proceedings of the 2016 conference of the North American chapter of the association for computational linguistics: human language technologies*, pages 1480–1489.

Tong Zhang. 2004. Solving large scale linear prediction problems using stochastic gradient descent algorithms. In *Proceedings of the Twenty-first International Conference on Machine Learning*, ICML '04, pages 116–, New York, NY, USA. ACM.

Annotation Process for the Dialog Act Classification
of a Taglish E-commerce Q&A Corpus

Jared Rivera, Jan Caleb Oliver Pensica,
Jolene Valenzuela, Alfonso Secuya, Charibeth Cheng
De La Salle University, Manila, Philippines
{jared_rivera, jan_pensica, jolene_valenzuela,
alfonso_secuya, charibeth.cheng}@dlsu.edu.ph

Abstract

With conversational agents or chatbots making up in quantity of replies rather than quality, the need to identify user intent has become a main concern to improve these agents. Dialog act (DA) classification tackles this concern, and while existing studies have already addressed DA classification in general contexts, no training corpora in the context of e-commerce is available to the public. This research addressed the said insufficiency by building a text-based corpus of 7,265 posts from the question and answer section of products on Lazada Philippines. The SWBD-DAMSL tagset for DA classification was modified to 28 tags fitting the categories applicable to e-commerce conversations. The posts were annotated manually by three (3) human annotators and preprocessing techniques decreased the vocabulary size from 6,340 to 1,134. After analysis, the corpus was composed dominantly of single-label posts, with 34% of the corpus having multiple intent tags. The annotated corpus allowed insights toward the structure of posts created with single to multiple intents.

1 Introduction

An essential part of social media is the messaging feature which is easily adopted due to its convenience and speed in comparison to other communication methods (Alison Bryant et al., 2006). In the Philippines, most online sellers prefer using social media as an e-commerce platform for their businesses for exactly this reason (Marcelo, 2018). However, for social media to be effective as an e-commerce platform, active participation of the seller and the customer in the conversation is required. A general drawback in e-commerce is the lack or unavailability of sales clerks (i.e. online shop moderators) to interact with customers online. This problem is commonly evident among solo retailers, which provides an opportunity for the use of conversational agents to act as sales clerks on behalf of these sellers (Bogdanovych et al., 2005). Taglish (Tagalog-English) is often comfortably used on Philippine social media, and since natural language is noted as the most natural means of communication between humans (Weischedel et al., 1989), interaction using Taglish as natural language, is seen as a feasible option to connect these conversational agents with Filipino customers online (Hill et al., 2015).

However, misunderstandings are common in conversational interactions, more so when an online platform is used and transactions are conducted online than in-person, and the problem may be more complex once a machine is on one end of the conversation. Despite its capability to participate in a conversation, conversational agents still fail to simulate and capture the essence of the full range of an intelligent human conversation (Hill et al., 2015). The identification of dialog acts in an utterance is therefore an important goal of any system aiming to properly establish intent among participants to understand a conversation.

In this work, we focus on collecting and annotating the dialog acts of queries within the domain of e-commerce, specifically from Lazada Philippines, building a corpora with dialog act annotations named LazadaQA-Taglish-7k. The dataset is open sourced in a public repository. [1]

2 Related Works

A dialog act (DA) represents the intention of a person's utterance (Austin and Urmson, 1962). According to Stolcke et al. (2000), DAs may be considered as a set of tags that classifies utterances according to a combination of pragmatic, semantic, and syntactic criteria. In addition, it is de-

---

[1] https://github.com/dlsucelt/lazadaQA

Proceedings of the Second Workshop on Economics and Natural Language Processing, pages 61–68
Hong Kong, November 4. ©2019 Association for Computational Linguistics

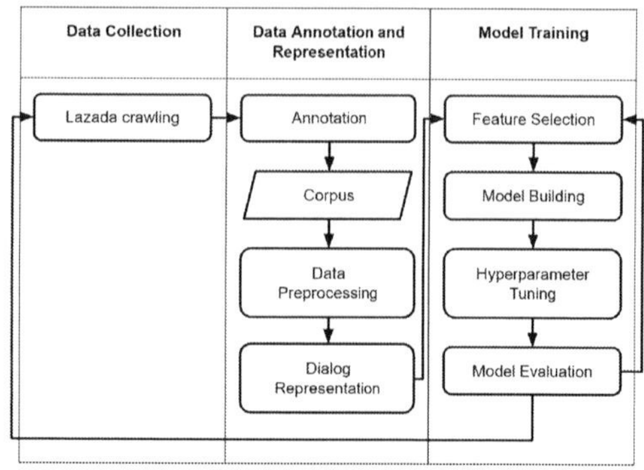

Figure 1: Flowchart of the Study

scribed to be a useful first level of dialog understanding to describe the structure of a conversation. There are four (4) commonly used publicly-available corpora that are usually used for training in DA classification: Switchboard (Godfrey et al., 1992), MapTask (Anderson et al., 1991), MRDA (Janin et al., 2003), and VERBMOBIL (Wahlster, 1993). It is noticeable that among all four corpora mentioned, there are no works that are applicable to the e-commerce setting. As of the time of writing there is only one e-commerce related work on DA classification by Meng and Huang (2017), which used a proprietary Chinese conversational dataset from a Chinese e-commerce service, however the dataset is not publicly available and details regarding its data collection were not specified. The lack of data for e-commerce dialogs motivated the building of the corpus for this work.

3 Methodology

The structure of the methodology for this study is illustrated in Figure 1. It is mainly divided into three phases, namely Data Collection, Data Annotation and Representation, and Model Training. Only the first two phases will be discussed, while the third phase will be briefly tackled in Section 5. Subsections that describe the steps per phase in detail follow.

3.1 Data Collection

For this work, 7,265 posts were scraped from the Q&A sections of products under the categories electronic devices and appliances, namely mobile phones, laptops, printers, and peripherals. These categories were chosen because of the nature of electronics which consists of many variation of

components and specifications that can possibly lead to a higher number of inquiries.

The data collection was done in two iterations: The first iteration crawled 1,967 posts under Audio Devices, and Computers and Laptops using Octoparse (Oct, 2018). The following iteration crawled an additional 5,298 posts under Printers, Mobile Accessories, and Audio Devices using a Python script that utilizes Selenium automated testing. Each post contains an utterance from a customer ("question") and a seller ("answer"), customer, seller, and time posted.

The final dataset contains posts from 39 unique sellers with 3,437 instances from the Audio Devices subcategory, 1,021 from Computers and Laptops, 1,365 from Mobile Accessories, and 1,442 from Printers.

3.2 Data Annotation

The annotation of data was done by three (3) individuals in parallel, guided by a list of tags. Final tags assigned to a post were decided by majority agreement such that if 2 up to 3 out of 3 annotators agreed that a post be assigned to a certain category, it will be assigned as such.

Each post could be classified with more than one (1) tag, thus presenting a Multilabel Classification Problem. This was addressed by transforming the labels by Binary Relevance. Labels were added to each post in their actual form (i.e. `Availability Inquiry`) and then converted to a binary vector with the length corresponding to all tags (28), with values 0 or 1 corresponding to whether a tag is applicable to the post.

The tagset used for identifying DAs was initially based on the SWBD-DAMSL tagset by Jurafsky et al. (1997) and then modified based upon common intents found in the posts. This led to the emergence of tags for the context of e-commerce. Tags used for the study are listed on Table 1 accompanied by examples where the tags apply.

The annotation was done in 4 iterations, with the tagset evolving over the course of the iterations. For the first iteration, 1,967 posts were crawled from Audio Devices and Computers and Laptops. The initial content included the initial dialog acts used in the Messenger dataset. `Discount Inquiry` was removed due to its similarity to `Promo Inquiry` in terms of definition.

In the second iteration, the non-occurring

Table 1: Tags used to annotate LazadaQA-Taglish-7k. Translations for Taglish phrases are provided in parentheses.

	Tag	Example
Inquiry	**Availability inquiry**	*Is the iPhone C still available for purchase?*
	Price inquiry	*kano ba IPHONEX?* *("how much is IPHONEX?")*
	Specification inquiry	*so wait.. ano ba features ng samsung* *("so wait.. what are the features of samsung")*
	Contact details inquiry	*Can I have your contact information?*
	Promo inquiry	*and are there any applicable promos that* *can be used for buying phones?*
	Delivery inquiry	*Do you ship?*
	Payment method inquiry	*Hi! I am inquiring about the Razer* *Blade Stealth, what are the means of payment?*
	Definition inquiry	*Ahm, itatanong ko lang haha. Ano yung ibig sabihin* *ng "unlocked"?* *("Ahm, I just wanted to ask haha. What does "unlocked" mean?")*
	Process inquiry	*Hi, nakita ko sa page niyo na may swap or sale* *for electronics, may I ask how the swap system works?* *("Hi, I saw that on your page there is swap or sale* *for electronics, may I ask how the swap system works?")*
	Product recommendation request	*Hi! What phone models do you recommend* *for a mid-ranged budget?*
	Request (action-directive)	*Please meet her near the university.*
	Clarification	*Under mobile networks, right?*
	Warranty inquiry	*wala po talaga sya warranty?* *("it really has no warranty?")*
	Inquiry (others)	*Is this legal, though?*
Complaint	**Service complaint**	*I even contacted you guys so many times already,* *but you guys never answer me properly.* *It is already so frustrating.*
	Product complaint	*Parang may problem ata sa hardware,* *di gumagana yung LTE ng SIM* *("It seems like there might be a problem with the hardware,* *the LTE of the SIM doesn't work")*
	Price complaint	*parang awa niyo na ito ba talaga price nito* *baka naman hindi bat ganun ang total pag* *add ko sa chart ko 1796* *("please is this really the price* *maybe its not why is the total like that* *after I add the price to my chart 1796")*
	Delivery complaint	*Excuse me i ordered iphone X* *bakit bato at sibuyas ang laman!!!!* *("Excuse me i ordered iphone X* *why is it full of rocks and onions!!!!")*
Expression	**Agreement / Accept / Yes-answer**	*Ok that would be fine.*
	Opening	*Hello*
	Thanking	*Ok thank you siz*
	Expression	*Huhu*
Transaction	**Purchase**	*I would like to order one iPhoneX* *through COD please*
	Order cancellation	*pwede ba cancel nlang iba nlang ooderin ko.* *("is it possible to cancel instead I will order something else.")*
	Return / Exchange / Refund	*if ever na may defect sya maam can i return it?* *("if ever it has a defect maam can i return it?")*
Other	**Backchannel**	*Ok wala na po ba tawad yan* *("Ok is there really no discount for that")*
	Follow-up	*wala pang reply ata sa tanong ko?* *("there might still be no reply to my question?")*
	Other	*Uy may nanalo na raw. :O* *("Uy they said someone won already. :O")*

tags `Swap` and `Negative / Reject / No-answer` were removed. In addition, the `Swap` tag was unique to e-commerce conversations on Messenger and is not a feature of Lazada Philippines. `Closing` was also removed due to the annotators experiencing difficulty in classifying such statements and the nature of QA postings being different from a linear conversational flow.

5,298 data points were annotated in the following iterations from Mobile Accessories, Audio Devices, and Printers. The third iteration saw an abundance of posts relating to product warranty, product return, exchange, or refunding, and order cancellations—all of which did not have corresponding tags in the tagset. The following tags were added to the tagset before the next iteration was started: `Warranty Inquiry`, `Price Inquiry`, `Price Complaint`, `Order Cancellation`, and `Return / Exchange / Refund`.

In addition, the tag `Delivery method inquiry` was renamed to `Delivery inquiry` as it was assumed for previous iterations that delivery-related inquiries only ask about possible methods of delivery (e.g. meet-up, courier, pick-up). There were no tags for certain instances of delivery-related inquiries such as asking for the estimated time of delivery, delivery fee, and about specific couriers in the tagset. Instead of adding new tags for each scenario, the tag `Delivery method inquiry` was made into a general tag that encapsulated all delivery-related inquiries.

Lastly, for the final iteration, the `Question (others)` tag was changed to `Inquiry` to be consistent with all inquiry tags.

The final tag distribution can be found in Table 2.

3.3 Inter-rater reliability

The Fleiss κ value, which extends the Cohen κ statistic to more than 2 annotators, was used to measure the inter-rater reliability of the annotators. For this study, the majority agreement was also measured among annotators as to decide the ground truth for DA labeling for the classification task in Section 5. The paradox of high-agreement (majority percentage) and low-reliability (κ value) was found to exist in this case. The computation was done through the following:

Let N be the number of messages, n be the number of annotators, k be the number of dialog act tags, i be the index of messages, j be the index of annotators, and n_{ij} as the number of annotators who assigned the j-th tag to the i-th message. First solve for p_j

$$p_j = \frac{1}{Nn}\sum_{i=1}^{N} n_{ij}, 1 = \sum_{j=1}^{k} p_j \qquad (1)$$

Table 2: LazadaQA-Taglish-7k Tag Distribution

Tag	Occurrence
Specification Inquiry	4143
Opening	971
Inquiry (others)	684
Thanking	679
Other	396
Product Complaint	389
Delivery Complaint	386
Delivery Inquiry	362
Availability Inquiry	351
Process Inquiry	347
Price Inquiry	265
Expression	175
Request	168
Service Complaint	131
Payment Method Inquiry	107
Warranty Inquiry	101
Return / Exchange / Refund	82
Price Inquiry	65
Contact Details Inquiry	65
Backchannel	61
Definition Inquiry	60
Follow-up	57
Price Complaint	51
Clarification	51
Product Recommendation Request	41
Purchase	33
Order Cancellation	30
Agreement / Accept / Yes-answer	16

where p_j is the proportion of all assignments to the j-th tag. Then compute for P_i

$$P_i = \frac{1}{n(n-1)}[(\sum_{j=1}^{k} n_{ij}^2) - (n)] \qquad (2)$$

where P_i shows how many annotator pairs are in agreement for all possible pairs. Next compute for P

$$P = \frac{1}{Nn(n-1)}(\sum_{i=1}^{N}\sum_{j=1}^{k} n_{ij}^2 - Nn) \qquad (3)$$

where P is the mean of the P_is. Then compute for P_e

$$P_e = \sum_{j=1}^{k} p_j^2 \qquad (4)$$

where P_e is the expected mean proportion of agreement. Lastly, plug the values of P and P_e into the following equation to get the value of κ:

$$\kappa = \frac{P - P_e}{1 - P_e} \qquad (5)$$

Table 3: Kappa Scores from Highest to Lowest Reliability

	Label	Kappa
1	Opening	0.9276
2	Payment method inquiry	0.9036
3	Thanking	0.8920
4	Warranty inquiry	0.8687
5	Availability inquiry	0.8491
6	Specification inquiry	0.8359
7	Price inquiry	0.7869
8	Product complaint	0.7628
9	Delivery complaint	0.7530
10	Contact details inquiry	0.7249
11	Delivery inquiry	0.7228
12	Promo inquiry	0.6499
13	Price complaint	0.5991
14	Service complaint	0.5296
15	Product recommendation request	0.5035
16	Process inquiry	0.4561
17	Expression	0.3760
18	Definition inquiry	0.3747
19	Order cancellation	0.3076
20	Other	0.2532
21	Backchannel	0.2392
22	Purchase	0.2321
23	Follow-up	0.2233
24	Request	0.2141
25	Clarification	0.1998
26	Agreement / Accept / Yes-answer	-0.0012
27	Return / Exchange / Refund	-0.0051
28	Inquiry (others)	-0.0379

where $1 - P_e$ defines the degree of agreement attainable above chance while $P - P_e$ stands for the actual degree of agreement achieved above chance. There are 2 possibilities for the value of κ, namely: $\kappa = 1$ means complete agreement while $\kappa = -1$ means complete disagreement.

The kappa scores can be found in Table 3.

3.4 Cleaning and Pre-processing

Before the data was used, empty rows were removed from the dataset. All of the posts were converted to lowercase, and terminal punctuation and emojis (digital icons supported by Unicode) were retained as we believe that they were important to the identification of intent behind a post (e.g. angry emoticons may signify complaints). Strings composed of non-separated terminal punctuation and emojis were split by spaces in order to reduce unigrams composed of the same character (e.g. "!!!" turn into '!','!','!'). Text normalization was also applied to the dataset, standardizing all numbers as the token "<num>", stopwords to "<st>", and rare words (words with 0.01% term frequency) to "<rr>". Many rare words normalized related to product titles and details that only occured in a single forum and had no bearing to

the intent of the post (e.g. earphones, airpods). This process significantly reduced the vocabulary size from 6,340 to 1,134.

4 Results and Discussion

The results of this study will mainly focus on the analysis of the crawled and annotated dataset, including figures to identify significant observations among the DAs.

4.1 Data Analysis

From Figure 2, while posts annotated with only one tag are dominant within the dataset, 34% of posts within the dataset are still classified under more than one tag, with a significant number of these posts having tag pairs (two tags).

Many observations can be made from Table 4 as to the possible relation between tags. Most of the tags under the inquiry group show similar words that are used in Taglish conversations implying a question (e.g. *"ba"*, a word in the Filipino vocabulary frequently used to ask for clarification) while also having words that relate to each individual tag's intent (e. g. "free" word is frequent among posts tagged as `Promo Inquiry`).

Under the complaint group however, most words are nouns pertaining to the order or item purchased, as topics of the complaint. The word *"lang"* ("only") also appears in complaint tags which may pertain to a lack of or of ill punctuality. There also appears to be an intersection between words used in complaints as well as inquiries, such as words *"lang"* ("only") and *"bakit"* ("why"). This suggests that complaints are often presented in inquiry form. The only tag with unique common words in contrast to the other complaint tags is `Price Complaint`, with many words relating to money such as *"mahal"* ("expensive"), "price", and "fee".

As for expression tags, most words are common among the tags such as "hi", "hello" and "thank". This could mean that most posts are structured to portrait all these intents, and posts that open a conversation could also close with an agreement or thanking expression.

For the transaction group, there is an appearance of words relating to an order or item, and imply a process (e.g. *"paano"* ("how"), "return", "order", "cancel"). While words such as "order" and "item" appear in the complaint group, the presence of expression tags, specifi-

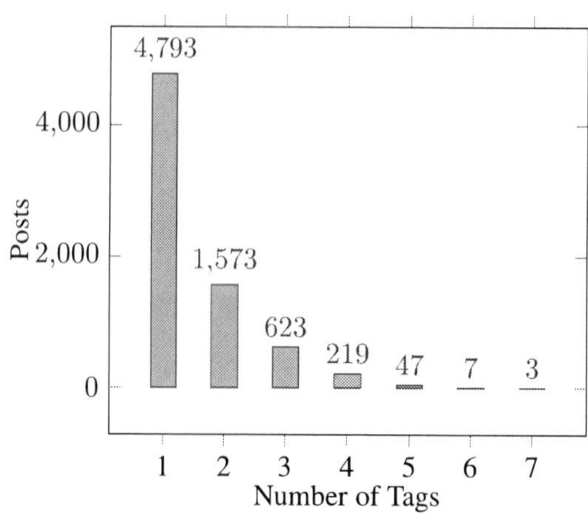

Figure 2: Multilabel Count Distribution

Table 4: Common Words used by Tagged Posts

	Tag	Common Words
Inquiry	Availability inquiry	*ba, available, meron, color, stock*
	Price inquiry	*ba, much, shipping, price, magkano, fee*
	Specification inquiry	*ba, pwede, compatible*
	Contact details inquiry	*ba, store, warranty, contact*
	Promo inquiry	*free, ba, shipping, sale*
	Delivery inquiry	*ba, order, day, ilang, delivery*
	Payment method inquiry	*cod, ba, installment, pwede, cash, delivery*
	Definition inquiry	*go, ano, jbl, ba*
	Process inquiry	*ba, order, paano, item*
	Product recommendation request	*pwede, printer, hi, item, one, thank*
	Request (action-directive)	*order, please, ba, item, thank, sana*
	Clarification	*ba, warranty, order, lang, hindi*
	Warranty inquiry	*warranty, ba, item, paano*
	Inquiry (others)	*ba, original, order, lang, bakit*
Complaint	Service complaint	*order, item, bakit, naman, wala*
	Product complaint	*lang, item, ba, hindi, bakit*
	Price complaint	*shipping, mahal, fee, price, bakit, lang*
	Delivery complaint	*order, bakit, wala, day, item*
Expression	Agreement / Accept / Yes-answer	*thank, ok, yes, opo*
	Opening	*hi, ba, hello, thank, lang, order, pwede*
	Thanking	*thank, order, ba, hello*
	Expression	*order, ba, naman, hindi, thank, sana*
Transaction	Purchase	*order, thank, hello, sana*
	Order cancellation	*order, cancel, lang*
	Return / Exchange / Refund	*item, paano, ba, order, return*
Other	Backchannel	*ba, naman, sabi, please*
	Follow-up	*hi, order, item, wala, follow*
	Other	*order, item, ba, lang*

cally, `Thanking` may differentiate the negative implications of a complaint from a transaction.

Lastly, tags classified under other, have no identifiable words distinguishable from the other tag categories since these tags hold a broader scope that cannot be properly defined. Tags, `Follow-Up` and `Backchannel`, both require the element of context to properly classify a post as such, while `Other` remains a catch-all tag that is given if a post cannot be classified under any other tag.

5 Application and Current Usage

The resulting corpus and annotations were used to create e-commerce dialog act classifiers. The best-

66

Table 5: Results from the best DA classification models as an application of this work.

| | SVM (BoW) | | MLP (TF-IDF) | |
	Train	Test	Train	Test
Accuracy	99.46%	99.07%	84.15%	83.58%
Precision	98.03%	96.19%	71.54%	68.26%
Recall	94.17%	89.56%	85.73%	79.71%
F1-score	95.97%	92.68%	75.17%	70.58%

performing machine learning model was a Support Vector Machine (SVM) that used Bag of Words (one-hot encoding) on the questions as features while the best-performing deep learning model was a Multilayer Perceptron (MLP) that used TF-IDF as features. A summary of the results for the best models from this phase of the study can be found on Table 5.

6 Conclusion

This study was able to collect a total of 7,265 posts from the Q&A sections of products in Lazada Philippines. The posts were from products under printers, speakers, and electronic devices and a Python script with Selenium automated testing. The entries contain a question (customer utterance), an answer (seller utterance), the customer, seller, and the timestamp for the post. The corpus was annotated manually by three (3) human annotators using a tagset of 28 dialog acts tailor-fit for e-commerce conversations which were based on the SWBD-DAMSL tagset by Jurafsky et al.. Analysis of the corpus revealed the multilabel nature of posts as well as intersections of common words and intent, within and among the tag groups. Finally, the LazadaQA-Taglish-7k provides a foundation for the use of Taglish in conversational agent interactions as it is the first e-commerce corpora of its kind in its language, which can be applied in the development of conversational agents in the said domain as well as other related fields.

References

2018. Octoparse.

J Alison Bryant, Ashley Sanders-Jackson, and Amber MK Smallwood. 2006. Iming, text messaging, and adolescent social networks. *Journal of Computer-Mediated Communication*, 11(2):577–592.

Anne H Anderson, Miles Bader, Ellen Gurman Bard, Elizabeth Boyle, Gwyneth Doherty, Simon Garrod, Stephen Isard, Jacqueline Kowtko, Jan McAllister, Jim Miller, et al. 1991. The HCRC Map Task Corpus. *Language and speech*, 34(4):351–366.

John Langshaw Austin and James Opie Urmson. 1962. *How to Do Things with Words. The William James Lectures Delivered at Harvard University in 1955.[Edited by James O. Urmson.].* Clarendon Press.

Anton Bogdanovych, SJ Simoff, Carles Sierra, and Helmut Berger. 2005. Implicit training of virtual shopping assistants in 3d electronic institutions. *e-commerce*.

John J Godfrey, Edward C Holliman, and Jane McDaniel. 1992. SWITCHBOARD: Telephone Speech Corpus for Research and Development. In *Acoustics, Speech, and Signal Processing, 1992. ICASSP-92., 1992 IEEE International Conference on*, volume 1, pages 517–520. IEEE.

Jennifer Hill, W. Randolph Ford, and Ingrid G. Farreras. 2015. Real conversations with artificial intelligence: A comparison between human—human online conversations and human—chatbot conversations. *Computers in Human Behavior*, 49:245–250.

Adam Janin, Don Baron, Jane Edwards, Dan Ellis, David Gelbart, Nelson Morgan, Barbara Peskin, Thilo Pfau, Elizabeth Shriberg, Andreas Stolcke, et al. 2003. The ICSI meeting corpus. In *Acoustics, Speech, and Signal Processing, 2003. Proceedings.(ICASSP'03). 2003 IEEE International Conference on*, volume 1, pages I–I. IEEE.

Daniel Jurafsky, Elizabeth Shriberg, and Debra Biasca. 1997. Switchboard-DAMSL labeling project coder's manual. *Technická Zpráva*, pages 97–02.

Patrizia C Marcelo. 2018. Most filipino merchants prefer social media as top e-commerce platform — survey. *BusinessWorld*.

Lian Meng and Minlie Huang. 2017. Dialogue Intent Classification with Long Short-Term Memory Networks. In *National CCF Conference on Natural Language Processing and Chinese Computing*, pages 42–50. Springer.

Andreas Stolcke, Klaus Ries, Noah Coccaro, Elizabeth Shriberg, Rebecca Bates, Daniel Jurafsky, Paul Taylor, Rachel Martin, Carol Van Ess-Dykema, and Marie Meteer. 2000. Dialogue act modeling for automatic tagging and recognition of conversational speech. *Computational linguistics*, 26(3):339–373.

Wolfgang Wahlster. 1993. Verbmobil. In *Grundlagen und anwendungen der künstlichen intelligenz*, pages 393–402. Springer.

Ralph Weischedel, Jaime Carbonell, Barbara Grosz, Wendy Lehnert, Mitchell Marcus, Raymond Perrault, and Robert Wilensky. 1989. White Paper on Natural Language Processing. In *Proceedings of the Workshop on Speech and Natural Language*, HLT

'89, pages 481–493, Stroudsburg, PA, USA. Association for Computational Linguistics.

Author Index